100 THINGS TO DO IN BOZEMAN BEFORE YOU DIE

I0807794

Big Mike and Pasque Flowers

100
THINGS TO DO IN
BOZEMAN
BEFORE YOU
DIE

AMY GRISAK

REEDY PRESS

Copyright © 2025 by Reedy Press, LLC
Reedy Press
PO Box 5131
St. Louis, MO 63139, USA
reedypress.com

No part of this publication may be reproduced or transmitted in any form or by any means, electronic or mechanical, including photocopy, recording, or any information storage and retrieval system, without permission in writing from the publisher.

Permissions may be sought directly from Reedy Press at the above mailing address or via our website at reedypress.com.

Library of Congress Control Number: 2024949384

ISBN: 9781681065106

Design by Jill Halpin

Cover photo courtesy of Amy Grisak

Unless otherwise noted, all photos are courtesy of the author or believed to be in the public domain.

Printed in the United States of America
25 26 27 28 29   5 4 3 2 1

We (the publisher and the author) have done our best to provide the most accurate information available when this book was completed. However, we make no warranty, guarantee, or promise about the accuracy, completeness, or currency of the information provided, and we expressly disclaim all warranties, express or implied. Please note that attractions, company names, addresses, websites, and phone numbers are subject to change or closure, and this is outside of our control. We are not responsible for any loss, damage, injury, or inconvenience that may occur due to the use of this book. When exploring new destinations, please do your homework before you go. You are responsible for your own safety and health when using this book.

DEDICATION

This book is dedicated to my husband, Grant; my sons, Samuel and John; and, of course, my “wittle bitty boy,” Zeke, who is my adventure sidekick.

CONTENTS

Sports and Recreation

Culture and History

Shopping and Fashion

View of Bozeman along the "M Trail"

ACKNOWLEDGMENTS

I want to sincerely thank everyone who answered my innumerable questions as I delved into the history, activities, and restaurants we often take for granted. This includes all the folks in the tourism realm who pointed me in the right directions when I was overwhelmed with the incredible opportunities Bozeman offers. They took the time to provide the details I needed to help me breathe life into the descriptions of all the wonderful businesses and activities available in this breathtaking area.

Of course, I must give Pandora Moore a huge thank-you for hiking, eating, and exploring all the cool stuff with me. It's way more fun to do these things with a friend! The same holds for Linda Barghultz. While we miss you in the neighborhood, I am happy to pick you up to grab breakfast anytime.

Meeting Leslie Kilgore, Stacie Harris, and Blythe Beaubien was also a treat during this project. Thank you for your infectious enthusiasm and recommendations. I look forward to getting together for hikes and other exciting activities!

I also want to offer my appreciation for the top-notch team at Reedy Press who amaze me with their impressive efficiency and professionalism through every step of this journey.

PREFACE

A vibrant, positive energy is palpable as soon as you near Bozeman. I speculate that this is how people felt over the centuries as they ventured into this expansive, lush valley fed by six rivers and surrounded by four mountain ranges. It is the land of possibilities.

For the Niitsitapi (Blackfeet), the Gallatin Valley is Pisatssaisskiitsi Omahksiikaawahkoi, the "Valley of the Flowers," as this area has long been a neutral meeting place for the Native Peoples, including the Apsáalooke (Crow), Tsetsêhesêstâhase and So'taa'eo'o (Northern Cheyenne), Ksanka (Kootenai), Sélish (Salish), Lakota and Dakota (Sioux), Nimíipuu (Nez Perce), Bannock, and Shoshoni tribes. The region is also where Sacajawea, Shoshoni guide for the Lewis and Clark Expedition, recognized the familiar landmarks of her childhood home that let her companions know they were on the right course.

Legendary mountain men like John Colter, hunter and guide on the Lewis and Clark Expedition, and Jim Bridger, the namesake of the Bridger Mountain Range, sought their fortunes by living off the land. The gold miners soon followed, staking their claims near Virginia City and Nevada City. These hearty souls set the stage for entrepreneurs such as John Bozeman and Nelson Story, who built the foundation for the town we know today.

Now, as the third-largest city in Montana, Bozeman offers recreational opportunities and a deep sense of community that call people to this bustling region. There are few other places in

Montana, especially with the amenities of Bozeman, where top-notch trails, fishing, and floating are within a short bike ride of downtown. It's why so many people visit and decide to move to the area.

Bozeman is busy, at least by Montana standards, but the trade-off is a thriving community arts and entertainment scene and phenomenal food. Gone are the days of salads made only with iceberg lettuce topped with ranch dressing—or blue cheese if you felt fancy. Now we can find almost any food and drink imaginable, as Bozeman attracts world-class culinary artists who bring us the best. From scrumptious breakfasts to those late-night bites, Bozeman has it all.

I hope you take this book as a jumping-off point to discover the world of possibilities Bozeman offers. We love the favorite activities and businesses we've known for decades, yet we look forward to the new arrivals who bring us the unique experiences that make Bozeman like no other place in Montana.

Creative Cocktail at Sky Shed

FOOD AND DRINK

1

START THE DAY

AT RISE AND SHINE CAFE & BAKERY

There is a reason people line up at Rise and Shine Cafe & Bakery. Rise and Shine offers home cooking at its best with their bread, homemade jams, and farm-fresh ingredients. They serve traditional breakfast plates of eggs, toast, and hash browns, and carb lovers can enjoy classic biscuits and gravy with hash browns. They also offer plenty of options for the keto folks, such as a breakfast bowl with eggs, bacon, ham, sausage, avocado, salsa, cheddar cheese, and sour cream. Their avocado toast shines with sprouts, feta cheese, and huckleberry hot honey drizzled over the top for a different twist on a trendy favorite. Their breakfast burritos include the standard Early Bird with scrambled eggs; hash browns; sausage, ham or bacon; along with cheddar cheese and salsa. Or opt for the hearty Dakota, which combines grilled beef, sautéed bell peppers, jalapeño jelly, and chipotle ranch. They even have a walk-up window to grab and take what you need to fuel your day.

4875 Jackrabbit Ln., 406-338-3921
riseandshinecafeandbakery.com

MORE AMAZING BREAKFAST OPTIONS

Western Cafe
Pull up a stool and enjoy traditional Montana fare at its finest.

443 E Main St., 406-587-0436
thewesterncafe.com

Jam!
They're known for their delicious twists on classic breakfast dishes, such as stuffed challah bread French toast and crab cake eggs Benedict.

25 W Main St., 406-585-1761
jamonmain.com

Main Street Overeasy
From egg dishes to pancakes to Mexican breakfasts, there is something for everyone.

9 E Main St., 406-587-3205
mainstreetovereasy.com

The Coffee Pot Bakery & Cafe
They are renowned for their cinnamon rolls, along with breakfast burritos, delicious quiches, baked goodies, and excellent coffee.

80795 Gallatin Rd., 406-586-2146
thecoffeepotbakery.com

Storm Castle Cafe
Enjoy ever-changing adaptions of their omelets, eggs Benedict, and French toast.

5 Tai Ln., 406-586-0395
stormcastlecafe.com

2

RECHARGE FROM BEAN TO BREW

AT GHOST TOWN COFFEE ROASTERS

Sitting down for a cup of coffee is a universal experience, and creating gathering places for the community is a central theme of Ghost Town Coffee Roasters. Their signature, craft-roasted coffee blends make this a favorite for coffee connoisseurs. The talented staff at Ghost Town focus on the entire coffee-making process, starting at the agricultural level and developing relationships with growers worldwide. They expertly roast the highest-quality, ethically sourced coffee beans in-house, creating coffees with specific flavor profiles and consistently exceptional standards. The foundation of their business has long been the wholesale distribution of these fine blends. Still, three locations in Bozeman offer their coffee in all its glory, along with a delicious array of home-baked pastries to complement the perfect cup of coffee. Because coffee is their life, Ghost Town offers classes in methods of coffee brewing, plus it is the place to go for all your coffee-making needs.

Bridger Center Cafe/Wholesale
104 Bridger Center Dr., Ste. A,
406-577-2662

One 11 Cafe
110 W Beall St., 406-534-0654
ghosttowncoffee.com

Black Olive Cafe
110 E Olive St., 406-577-2400

MORE COFFEE SHOPS TO KICK-START YOUR DAY

Wild Joe*s Coffee Spot
Partnering with many Montana-made producers, including with Kalispell Kreamery's "cream on top" whole milk for their milk-based drinks, makes Wild Joe*s a Montana experience in itself.

18 W Main St., 406-586-1212
wildjoescoffee.com

Revamped Coffee Co.
Fun and whimsical, "Montana's only spooky coffee hut" features entertainingly odd Halloween themes backed by terrific coffee in a wide array of flavors. Grab a breakfast burrito to fuel the day's adventures.

403 Jackrabbit Ln., Belgrade, 602-565-4255

The Buzz Coffee Bar
An uplifting atmosphere and tasty coffee are great reasons to swing into Buzz Coffee in Belgrade.

81 8th St., Belgrade, #1, 406-595-8634
thebuzzcoffeebarmt.com

Rockford Coffee Roasters
Their spacious and inviting space offers equally excellent coffee and pastries—especially their scones. Plus, they make phenomenal chai!

18 E Main St., 406-556-1053
rockfordcoffee.com

3

ENJOY THE FLAVOR OF PARIS AT AURORE FRENCH BAKERY

There would be world peace if everyone could daily partake of Aurore's heavenly sourdough breads, pastries, and viennoiseries. Aurore Adam, hailing from Paris, brings the French baking tradition to Bozeman. She imports Les Grands Moulins de Paris flour and French butter to create the bakery's authentic masterpieces. The light-as-a-feather, flaky croissants melt in your mouth, and the pain au chocolat and croissant Forêt Noire are perfect for those craving sweetness. Pair with a café Americano, espresso, or latte made from Kawa coffee roasted in Paris, and you cannot help but be happy. On the savory side, they serve Croque Monsieur featuring egg, ham, and béchamel sauce, topped with melted Swiss cheese on sourdough bread. They also offer baguette sandwiches, including the Végétarien as a meatless option. Don't forget to take home baguettes or any of their sourdough bread selections to enjoy until your next visit for more food for the soul.

141 W Baxter Ln., Unit 13, 406-581-1092
aurorebakery.com

TIP

Aurore is open from Thursday to Sunday. Arrive early, especially on weekends.

OTHER EXCEPTIONAL BAKERIES

Wild Crumb
They have an overwhelming (in a good way) selection of exceptional breads and baked goods.

600 N Wallace Ave., 406-579-3454
wildcrumb.com

Vienne
Vienne features remarkable artisan breads and baked goods.

101 S Wallace Ave., 406-624-6040
viennemt.com

4

PICK UP AN AWARD WINNER
AT THE PICKLE BARREL

When locals look for a sandwich, they head to the Pickle Barrel, a fixture near the Montana State University campus for over 50 years. Alums and visitors return year after year for their hot cheese steak variations, ranging from a classic sandwich with steak, grilled onions, and Monterey Jack cheese, to the Blue Streak sandwich that adds tangy blue cheese. MSU fans favor the Bobcat Special made with roast beef, turkey, Swiss, and Monterey Jack or the Italian, a longtime favorite, which features prosciutto cotto, Italian salami, and provolone cheese, for cold sandwich options to take with them. Although known for their sandwiches, the Pickle Barrel also creates equally robust salads, offering grilled steak and chicken options. They are open seven days a week, and stay open until 10 p.m. during the weekdays, ideal for study breaks or for those who want to experience one of Bozeman's favorite sandwiches.

809 W College St., 406-587-2411
picklebarrelmt.com

5

FILL UP
AT FEED CAFÉ

Built in 1898 as part of the Henry Kirk family farm, the eye-catching red barn on Main Street has lived many lives; most recently, it houses one of Bozeman's favorite eateries. The team at Feed Café respects its agricultural roots and fosters close relationships with local producers to bring the freshest, highest-quality local ingredients to their kitchens. Open seven days a week, Feed's friendly staff takes pride in offering delicious classic and specialty breakfasts, such as the popular Panzanella, topped with croutons, arugula, sausage, goat-milk feta cheese, and a sun-dried tomato balsamic vinaigrette, finished with two sunny-side-up eggs. For lunch, try hot sandwiches and hearty salads like the Harissa Chicken with avocado, honey-roasted carrots, spiced pumpkin seeds, and organic greens topped with a yogurt dressing. The staff is knowledgeable and accommodating when it comes to gluten-free options. Besides offering gluten-free bread, the kitchen takes great care to ensure safe meals.

1530 W Main St., 406-219-2630
feedcafebozeman.com

TIP

During the warmer months, enjoy the outdoor seating, and feel free to bring your dog to join you on the patio with complimentary water for them while you enjoy your meal.

6

SHOW UP HUNGRY
AT ROOST FRIED CHICKEN

Featured on the Food Network's *Diners, Drive-Ins and Dives* with Guy Fieri, this perfectly seasoned, buttermilk-drenched fried chicken offers comfort food at its finest. You can choose boneless or bone-in chicken, served as traditional Southern fried chicken or with "sweet or heat" options. Their chicken and waffles epitomizes a satisfying meal, with this favorite combination served with honey pecan butter that you'll want to eat with a spoon. Roost also offers several sandwich options, along with lighter salads featuring fried or pulled chicken. They keep kids in mind with a menu all their own, but you have to realize that this will seriously step up their chicken nugget expectations! As yummy as their chicken is, their Southern-inspired sides, such as collard greens, grits, and fried okra, can be a meal on their own. Roost sits next to Feed Cafè, and their building—the former chicken house from Kirk Farm—pays homage to the area's rich agricultural history.

1520 W Main St., 406-404-1475
roostfriedchicken.com

7

RAISE A PINT
AT VALHALLA MEADERY

Make a toast with the "nectar of the gods" at Valhalla Meadery, one of only two meaderies in Montana. Mead, a fermented honey beverage, originated roughly 8,000 years ago, with the earliest evidence found in China from 6500 BCE. These days, it is better known as the Vikings' preferred drink. Valhalla Meadery crafts this alcohol using pristine Montana water and locally sourced honey, primarily from Smoot Honey, a multi-generational Montana apiary, as well as from producers within the Gallatin Valley. These artisans elevate the experience with interesting combinations such as beet or ginger meads or a wildflower mead infused with vanilla and cinnamon. Because mead tends to be on the sweeter side, an excellent option is the drier, sparkling Shield Maiden, perfect for a hot summer day. Their tasting room offers a flight of four four-ounce samples. Discover your favorites and take home a bottle or two. Continuing the Scandinavian theme, they have a hearty and delectable selection of Swedish meatballs, smoked and cured meats, pickled vegetables, home-baked bread, refreshing salads, and seasonal desserts.

875 Bridger Dr., Unit B, 406-577-2383
valhallabozeman.com

8

SIP YOUR FAVORITE BREW
AT A BOZEMAN BREWERY

Locally referred to as "The Bozone," the Bozeman Brewing Company is the oldest brewery in Bozeman. What started as a home-brewing hobby became a local favorite, well-known for its exceptional sours, among other well-crafted options. When sours became a thing in the beer world, Bozeman Brewing stepped up to the plate with 285 oak barrels in their basement, known as the "Underground," to create these small-batch recipes, making each glass unique. Beyond delicious sours, they have an impressive year-round lineup of IPAs, ales, and porters, along with much-anticipated seasonal flavors such as Sad Snowman, a Vienna-style lager, and the Oktoberfest-style lager Harvestfest. While they are all about creating top-notch beers, they take sustainability seriously. Their solar panels produce 30 percent of their annual power needs; they send their spent grain to a local ranch as a treat for the cows; and their Sunday FUNday supports local charitable organizations. They even created the EcoStar IPA to celebrate their EcoStar award. Head to the tasting room to find your favorite to take on your next adventure.

504 N Broadway, 406-585-9142
bozemanbrewing.com

MORE LOCAL BREWERIES

Mountains Walking

Mountains Walking offers an impressive variety, from Twisted Karma, a raspberry-infused sour, to Nice Fella, a more traditional pilsner. Also, keep an eye open for the New Hokkaido label, the "phantom brewery" that features Japanese-inspired rice lagers and IPAs, along with refreshing craft seltzers.

422 N Plum Ave., 406-219-3480
mountainswalking.com

Bridger Brewing

Bridger Brewing has one location near MSU and a newer, larger facility in Three Forks that can accommodate 2,000 people on its lawn for outdoor events. They are known for crafting a tasty Premo Pilsner, along with a wide selection of stouts, ales, and specialty sodas, including ginger beer and root beer, for something refreshingly different.

Bozeman
1609 S 11th Ave., 406-587-2124

Three Forks
75 Vigilante Way, 406-587-2124
bridgerbrewing.com

MAP Brewing

The views from the beer garden are as spectacular as the wide selection of brews. Flavors such as the Watermelon Crawl start on a sweet note, while Strange Cattle adds pineapple to the mix. Grab one of their marvelous burgers or wraps and a side of poutine, a Canadian-inspired dish of french fries and cheese curds smothered in gravy.

510 Manley Rd., 406-587-4070
mapbrewing.com

COOL OFF
WITH GENUINE ICE CREAM

Any day is made better with a generous scoop of Genuine Ice Cream in all its frozen, delicious goodness. They make their ice cream locally in small batches with Montana-sourced dairy products, create their own fruit purees for the fruit flavors, and steep lavender blossoms in the ice cream base for the lemon honey flavor. Even the waffle cones and cookies are baked in-house.

At their central location, choose between 10 standard flavors along with a couple of rotating options. Whether you're a fruit lover or prefer the richness of chocolate, you'll find a flavor to make you happy. Because huckleberry is a must-have during a Montana visit, try their version with locally harvested huckleberries and a touch of lemon for a sweet-tart flavor that perfectly refreshes in the summer. The made-from-scratch salted caramel and chocolate pretzel combination is hard to beat for sheer decadence, although the peanut butter Butterfinger flavor might rival the experience. Genuine Ice Cream is available at its retail location or in many local eateries and grocery stores.

605 W Peach St., Unit 101, 406-624-6633
genuineicecream.com

TIP

Their retail location is open until 11 p.m. during the summer and is perfect for an evening treat after a hike.

10

SAVOR EVERY BITE
AT LA CHÂTELAINE CHOCOLAT CO.

When you step inside La Châtelaine, you feel like you're visiting a chocolatier in a small French town. Rows upon rows of delicate chocolate creations look almost too good to eat—but *almost* is the key word. The artisans at La Châtelaine handcraft approximately 40 different types of chocolate daily using French and Swiss chocolate. Founders and husband-and-wife team Wlady and Shannon Growchowski trained in Paris, France, and use their extensive experience to create combinations found nowhere else in Montana. It's impossible to pick a favorite, but a few standouts are worth mentioning. The sea salt caramel absinthe, with its green design on top, looks as beautiful as it tastes. The pain d'épice, a dark chocolate ganache with ginger, cloves, cinnamon, black pepper, anise, and honey, offers a surprising yet delightful combination. The helpful staff will provide recommendations to help you make the most flavorful choices. Be sure to bring a selection home to enjoy later or share with friends.

110 S Rouse Ave., 406-522-5440 or 866-522-5440
chatelainechocolate.com

TIP

In addition to its primary location, a small La Châtelaine Chocolat Co. shop is conveniently located within the lobby of the Baxter Hotel at 105 W Main St.

11

PULL INTO
RED TRACTOR PIZZA

You can easily spot this local favorite by the eye-catching red tractor parked near the entrance and the tables on the shaded patio. They tout "New York Style brick-oven pizzas with a Bozeman spin," and whatever they're doing, they're doing it right. The delectable thin crust with slightly crunchy edges is perfect to fold in half for a mouthful of the most surprisingly delicious topping combinations. The Spicy Chicken Cacciatore adds a little heat, but not too much, to homemade red sauce, along with tender chicken, mushrooms, caramelized onions, and red peppers. The Waldorf pizza balances everything beautifully with apples, bacon, and blue cheese for a savory and sweet combination. There is so much to love, but what makes Red Tractor Pizza special is its focus on high-quality, often locally sourced ingredients, from the flours they use for the crust to organic, nitrate-free pepperoni. For dietary concerns, they have sprouted-grain and gluten-free crusts, plus plenty for those looking for nondairy or vegan options.

1007 W Main St., 406-359-1999
redtractorpizza.com

TIP

Besides fantastic pizza, cold beer, and yummy Italian wines, head to Red Tractor Pizza for live music four nights a week, making nearly any visit a special occasion.

MORE PIZZA IN BOZEMAN

Pizza Campania
Classic Neapolitan pizzas baked in a wood-fired oven make even Italian-born pizza lovers happy.

1285 N Rouse Ave., 406-404-1270
pizzacampania.net

Sidewall Pizza Company
It's hard to pick a favorite of their 20 varieties (or create your own) on their hand-tossed crust.

207 W Olive St., 406-570-0730
sidewallpizzabozeman.com

12

TRY A NEW TWIST ON TRADITIONAL FAVORITES

AT WHISTLE PIG KOREAN

When most people think of Montana, they do not envision authentic Korean cuisine, but you'll fall head over heels for Chef Emma Woods's creations. Named for one of her favorite cute furry animals, Whistle Pig is where traditional Korean cuisine meets high-quality Montana ingredients in a modern, fresh, and vibrant atmosphere. Start with kimbap (made with your choice of kimchi or bulgogi beef), sweet and spicy Korean-style chicken wings, or a delicious lion's mane mushroom and scallion pancake. (Add a little kimchi on the side to make it extra yummy.) Customize the bibimbap (Korean rice bowl) by adding chicken, pork, beef, or tofu to a base packed with spinach, locally grown mushrooms, mung beans, zucchini, and an over-easy egg; all served over rice with spicy gochujang (fermented pepper paste). Enjoy entrées like the super tender galbi, barbecued short ribs, or japchae bap made with sweet potato noodles, vegetables, and rice. The menu also offers many meatless options for vegan and vegetarian guests. Pair your meal with beer, wine, sake, or soju, a Korean distilled liquor made from rice.

25 N Willson Ave., Ste. A, 406-404-1224
whistlepigkorean.com

ADDITIONAL ASIAN-INSPIRED CUISINE

Tanoshii

Offering a twist on the classic buns, curry, and ramen, including a delectable Wagyu Yakisoba, the creative team turns it up a notch combining crispy Okonomiyaki waffles with Korean fried chicken. With its Izakaya-inspired atmosphere, this is the place to gather friends to hang out and share plates and stories of the day.

113 E Main St., 406-219-3984
tanoshiimt.com

Shan

"Shan" is the Chinese character meaning mountain, and the culinary team at Shan in Bozeman fuses Montana-produced ingredients into dishes inspired by the cuisine of northern Thailand and southwestern China. Barbecue, curries, stews, noodles, and meals from the wok create regionally unique cuisine found nowhere else in Montana—and maybe the world.

109 E Oak St., #1J, 406-577-2222
shanrestaurants.com

Sweet Chili Asian Bistro

Sweet Chili Asian Bistro brings together traditional Asian-inspired cuisine incorporating local bison, roasted duck, lamb chops, sea bass, and Oro salmon in memorable dishes. Every dish is a delight, although the Drunken Noodles Bison is a particular favorite.

101 E Main St., Ste. 1E, 406-582-1188
sweetchilibistro.com

SAMPLE THE MANY FLAVORS OF HARD CIDER

AT LOCKHORN CIDER HOUSE

Cozy up next to the fire on the outdoor patio while sipping a handcrafted cider on a cool autumn evening for the perfect end to your day. But there is no need to wait until fall to find this relaxing atmosphere. The folks at Lockhorn Cider House take cider making to the next level with 14 varieties on tap, featuring creative flavor combinations such as Gallatin Grapefruit Mint, a perfect way to quench your thirst on a hot summer afternoon. For traditionalists, enjoy the light and crisp Bridger Bone Dry or the renowned Newtown Pippin Cider, a well-known heritage apple variety. Take full advantage of the unique flavors of Montana with Flathead Cherry, incorporating fermented cherries grown around Flathead Lake, and Montana McIntosh, honoring the Bitterroot Valley's favorite apple.

In the fall, locals donate roughly 25,000 pounds of apples for their Backyard Blend, which varies yearly but always produces a delightful result. Pair the cider with local artisan cheeses, fruits, bison sausage, or a delicious apple affagoto. All of their drinks are gluten-free, for those looking for options.

21 S Wallace Ave., 406-580-9098
lockhornhardcider.com

FIND YOUR PERFECT PAIRING
AT PLONK

Plonk pairs creative cocktails or wine with ingenious culinary creations, mastering high-level techniques for marvelous results. Named after a British colloquialism for "cheap wine," Plonk is the opposite of anything middling. This wine and cocktail bar brings out the best in every aspect of the experience. Many of their cocktails are made with house-infused spirits, such as the G.F.C. with ginger vodka, basil, and a lemon–lime ginger simple. For an alcohol-free option, try a "zero-proof" drink like Easy Street, made with a combination of muddled fruit, a berry aperitif, fresh lemon–lime, and pomegranate. Even though your feet remain in Bozeman, you can tour the world with their wine selection and the finest champagnes. They prepare the food at the same level of excellence, including grilled venison chops, sweet potato gnocchi, and their outstanding vegan dark chocolate cheesecake.

29 E Main St., 406-587-2170
plonkwine.com

TIP

For an intimate gathering, book Plonk's wine cellar for a curated experience including a four- or seven-course meal and handpicked wine pairings.

TRAVEL THE CULINARY WORLD
WITH BOZEMAN'S FOOD-TRUCK SCENE

Summer days in Montana are gloriously long. After hiking or exploring the area, it's not unusual to make it back into town after 9 p.m. only to find many restaurants closed. Thankfully, Bozeman's food-truck scene is hopping with various food choices at your fingertips. For grab-and-go tacos, find El Rodeo in the parking lot at 509 North Seventh Avenue or look for Ramiere's at a popular food-truck pod at 319 North Seventh Avenue (near Mattress King). In this same pod, you'll find fabulous Lebanese cuisine at the Shawarma Bus as well as Schu Dogs, where you can eat bison brats and other yummy sausage dishes. If you want a good burger, Cholm's Burgers has you covered. Or savor the empanadas or other authentic Venezuelan dishes at La Vaca Mariposa.

The Bozeman Food Truck Park features food trucks in a family-friendly atmosphere at a convenient location. There is plenty of seating, along with firepits for chilly evenings and kids' activities and games.

1804 W Babcock St., 406-646-6789
bozemanfoodpark.com

16

SAVOR THE FINEST CULINARY CREATIONS
AT FEAST

If you are looking for something completely different, make a reservation at Feast. Aptly named because Feast's cuisine steps beyond a typical culinary experience into the world of visual art by using food as a delicious medium to create gorgeous plates. Focusing on complex flavors and beautiful presentation, their meals are a celebration of good food. The restaurant has an open and airy seating area with high walls and pressed-tin ceilings providing a welcoming feeling for a fine-dining experience. Their ever-changing menu has a few highlights, including the raw bar featuring ceviche, sashimi, oyster dishes, and Bison Carpaccio with thinly sliced, melt-in-your-mouth bison served with grilled crostini you'll find nowhere else. Feast flies in fresh seafood daily to create inspired dishes such as seared black grouper in a hazelnut pesto that is paired with a locally sourced seasonal salad flavored with fresh herbs. Or, for the terrestrial lovers, their Montana Wagyu grilled hangar steak from the Great Alone Cattle Company should not be missed.

270 W Kagy Blvd., Ste. C, 406-577-2377
feastbozeman.com

17

APPRECIATE THE PROCESS
AT BOZEMAN SPIRITS DISTILLERY

The award-winning Bozeman Spirits Distillery brings the finest quality liquor to downtown Bozeman with its Montana-inspired flavors. Sip the clean, fresh Cold Spring Huckleberry Vodka or try their signature Huckleberry Press with huckleberry vodka, lime, ice, and a few berries for garnish, creating the ultimate summer drink. Bozeman Spirits offers a well-rounded menu of high-quality liquors, including Old Faithful Bourbon, Prairie Schooner Barrel Aged Rum, Hell Roaring Cinnamon Whiskey, and Arrestado Agave Spirit, the secret ingredient for making your best margarita ever. Join a distillery tour to discover the magic behind the scenes, including learning how the glimmering 300-gallon traditional copper pot is used to create these exceptional spirits. The tour includes a flight of four spirits, but you don't have to join a tour to sample their styles. Order a flight to decide which ones you want to bring home.

121 W Main St., 406-577-2155
bozemanspirits.com

OTHER EXCELLENT DISTILLERIES

Dry Hills Distillery
Dry Hills Distillery creates true Montana spirits using wheat and potatoes from their fifth-generation family farm.

106 Village Center Ln., 406-624-6713
dryhillsdistillery.com

Wildrye Distilling
Wildrye Distilling is known for bourbon made from super-sweet corn raised on their multi-generational Montana farm as well as for several other spirits with local ingredients.

111 E Oak St., Ste. 1E, 406-577-2288
wildryedistilling.com

18

STOP IN FOR A STEAK

AT STACEY'S OLD FAITHFUL BAR & STEAKHOUSE

It's worth the half-hour drive to Gallatin Gateway for some of the best steaks in the area. In 1963, Stacey and Phyllis Crosby transformed the establishment from a local bar and regionally famous brothel into the place to be for dancing and a rowdy time welcoming cowboys and students alike. Stories abound of horses ridden across the dance floor and plenty of shenanigans. Now Stacey's daughter, Toni, operates the beloved business, continuing the legacy with excellent quality steaks, bison tenderloins, burgers, and hot sandwiches. For an authentic Montana experience, try Rocky Mountain oysters with cocktail sauce. And to help maintain Stacey's long tradition as a local watering hole, order a cold beer or a straight whiskey at the beautiful, ornately carved back bar that gives the place the old country watering hole atmosphere. It feels like stepping onto an old Western movie set. Music and dancing remain at the heart of Stacey's, so keep up with their weekly events to dance off all the good food they have to offer.

300 Mill St., Gallatin Gateway, 406-763-4425
staceysbar.com

SPEND A SPECIAL EVENING
AT BLACKBIRD

Created from the love and appreciation of authentic, delicious meals, Blackbird elevates the flavors of Montana. The open kitchen concept is a showpiece in and of itself, with the brick, wood-fired oven at the heart of the space. Taking the form of multiple courses, the culinary talents of Blackbird's chefs turn colorful, fresh vegetables into extraordinary works of art. Their homemade pasta—the kind that has the perfect firmness when you bite into it, yet seemingly melts together with the flavors of the dish—is renowned. And the presentations of various cuts of meat, ranging from locally raised lamb or bison, highlight the meal. Their pizza selection also impresses guests. The crust has a light, satisfying texture, with flavor imparted from the wood-fired oven. Try the classic Margherita topped with tomatoes, basil, and hand-stretched mozzarella, or the Salsiccia with fennel sausage, sweet onion, and Italian grana pandano. To round out the meal, guests will find the perfect accompaniment from their respectable beer and wine list, along with a few nonalcoholic options such as lemonade or a lovage tonic.

140 E Main St., 406-920-1751
blackbirdkitchen.com

20

EXPERIENCE THE BEST SEAT IN BOZEMAN

AT SKY SHED

Situated at the top of the Kimpton Armory Hotel Bozeman, visit Sky Shed to enjoy the outstanding views of the Bridgers and Spanish Peaks and the vibrant energy of downtown from the tallest building in Bozeman. Designed by renowned architect Fred F. Willson, who gave the front a 1920s Art Deco style, the building was constructed in 1941 to house the 163rd Regiment of the Montana National Guard. For years, the building sat abandoned until it was given new life as a nine-story luxury hotel and became a welcoming home base for Bozeman guests. Sky Shed crowns the building. This remarkable space is perfect for enjoying a cocktail and small bites served tapas style with little between you and the stars. During the warm months, Summer Soirée Rooftop Dance Parties bring people to the top of the building for an eclectic array of music, and the private firepit is available for special gatherings. In the winter, the Snow Shed creates a magical space with the magical ambiance of living in a giant snow globe.

24 W Mendenhall St., 406-551-7703
skyshedbar.com

TIP

Swing by Kimpton Armory Hotel to visit the Tune Up Basement Bar for excellent drinks, small bites, and live music in the former location of the military music room, or head to Fielding's for breakfast and lunch. Both are accessible via separate entrances on West Mendenhall Street, so there is no need to go through the lobby.

The Waiting
Credit The Waiting LLC

MUSIC AND ENTERTAINMENT

IMMERSE YOURSELF IN THE MUSIC
OF THE BOZEMAN SYMPHONY

For over 50 years, the Bozeman Symphony and Symphonic Choir have delighted Gallatin County residents and visitors from throughout the world with their premier lineup of musical ability. The highly talented musicians bring to life the works of classical composers such as Dvořák, Tchaikovsky, Bach, and Beethoven. The Symphonic Choir gives us goose bumps with their powerful voices, whether at the Christmas concert or performing Carl Orff's deeply moving *Carmina Burana*. The six concerts of their classical series bring world-class musical artists to their audience. One of the objectives of the Bozeman Symphony is to introduce exceptional musical performances to everyone, and family-friendly concerts, such as those featuring the familiar scores of movie composer John Williams, spark the love of live music in all ages. Their performances occur in the Willson Auditorium on 404 East Main Street. Built in 1937, the expansive building is another easily recognizable design of architect Fred F. Willson, who was responsible for many of the historic buildings within Bozeman, and originally served as Gallatin County High School.

402 E Main St., Ste. 202, 406-585-9774
bozemansymphony.org

TIP

Engage the kids at Symphony Storytime, held at the Bozeman Public Library (626 E Main St.), where they have a chance to listen to stories and enjoy a hands-on experience with the instruments that create this musical magic.

ENJOY THE DRAMA OF MONTANA SHAKESPEARE IN THE PARKS

"All the world's a stage, and all the men and women merely players. They have their exits and their entrances; And one man in his time plays many parts." These esteemed words of the venerated bard William Shakespeare invite all of us to experience his works, which have touched the souls of generations during the annual performances of Shakespeare in the Parks since 1973. Every summer, talented actors bring Shakespeare's comedies and tragedies free of charge to communities throughout Montana, Wyoming, Idaho, North Dakota, and Washington. Held outdoors, under the beautiful Montana sky, local artists are often featured in opening acts before the troupe breathes life into the immortal characters of Shakespeare's sharp-witted and enthralling stories. In early June, Bozeman hosts performances at the Duck Pond Grove, a beloved space and well-known Montana State University–campus fixture.

shakespeareintheparks.org

TIP

Bring a picnic dinner and stretch out on a blanket to experience Shakespeare with a Montana twist.

TAKE YOUR SEAT
AT THE ELLEN THEATRE

Walking into the Ellen Theatre transports you back to the day when the grand space epitomized culture in the burgeoning town of Bozeman. This elaborate structure was built in 1919 by the sons of Nelson Story and named for their mother, Ellen, the family's matriarch. At this time, Bozeman's population hovered around 6,000 people, while the Ellen Theatre held around 750 guests—over a tenth of the population of the town! Gilded plaster carvings and ornate fixtures adorn the towering walls and high ceiling, framing the curtained stage. Private boxes on either side of the performance area once gave privileged patrons the best seats in the house. Still, now, after recent renovations, the entire facility combines comfort and excellent views of the 270-plus performances offered throughout the year as it remains the center of entertainment well into this new century.

17 W Main St., 406-585-5885
theellentheatre.com

TIP

One of the most popular events is PechaKucha, an international storytelling platform in which participants have 400 seconds to tell their stories using 20 slides that progress every 20 seconds. Offered in the spring and fall, it's a terrific way to bring the community together on a grand scale!

FIND YOUR INNER THESPIAN
AT VERGE THEATER

Does the stage call to you? Even if you've never delved into the acting realm, the talented performers at Verge Theater open their arms to welcome you on your journey. From adults and teens to even school-age kids who move effortlessly between imagination and reality, the Verge staff creates an encouraging environment for every level of acting. Each course of classes wraps up with a showcase to highlight the performers' newly honed talents. Even if stepping onto the stage isn't on your bucket list, watch their well-produced, thought-provoking productions featuring exceptional local talent. Located within the Emerson Center for Arts and Culture, the intimate space can seat approximately 50 people, and, as a bonus, serves as an art gallery providing space for local artists to exhibit their work. In an effort to include everyone, they put forth a "pay as you wish" rate for their performances.

111 S Grand Ave., Ste. 107 C, 406-602-3131
vergetheater.com

BE ENTHRALLED
BY MONTANA BALLET COMPANY'S *THE NUTCRACKER* PERFORMANCE

The holiday season begins with the Christmas classic, Tchaikovsky's *The Nutcracker*, the tale of a young girl who is smitten with a nutcracker who turns into a prince and battles the Mouse King and his minions on Christmas Eve, performed by the Montana Ballet Company. The company brings world-class dance to Bozeman, engaging professional and international dancers, and provides exceptional classical training for Bozemanites. Besides the beloved Christmas production, they have a full-length classical performance often featuring stories such as *Swan Lake* or *A Midsummer Night's Dream* during spring productions. The Academy is the educational branch of the company. Its goal is to engage dancers of all ages and skill levels to teach them the foundations of dance, especially during their annual Dancing Under the Big Sky, a two-week dance-intensive workshop.

2304 N 7th Ave., Ste. C-3, 406-582-8702
montanaballet.org

TIP

For a special event surrounding *The Nutcracker*, sign up for Tea with Clara, a high tea event at the Baxter Ballroom. It's a perfect opportunity to dress up and enjoy a dainty cup of tea and a few tasty bites before visiting a few of the cast members onstage.

CELEBRATE MUSICAL ARTISTS
AT LIVE FROM THE DIVIDE

Historic buildings and music from the heart that nourishes the soul go hand in hand, making a performance at Live from the Divide an event you won't soon forget. The cozy space transforms into what feels like a private concert for 50 fortunate audience members, who experience an eclectic array of talented songwriters and musicians firsthand. The lineup is truly as diverse as America, showcasing musical artists in forms ranging from a hip-hop pianist to folk/Americana or Latin pop artists. Live from the Divide brings together the people crafting the songs that resonate deeply within our world experiences and introduces Bozeman to songwriters heard nowhere else. Built in 1905, the beautiful brick building, impossible to miss, stands as Bozeman's first cold storage for produce shipped into the region by railroad. Now, it is a much warmer space as talented musicians and an appreciative audience share this unique experience together.

627 E Peach St., 406-624-3321
livefromthedivide.com

CELEBRATE BIRDS OF PREY
AT THE BRIDGER RAPTOR FESTIVAL

The largest golden eagle migration in the United States occurs between September and November above the skies of the Bozeman area, and everyone has a front-row seat during the Bridger Raptor Festival. To celebrate the migration of between 2,000 and 3,500 raptors, for two days in early October, the Bridger Raptor Festival offers activities and presentations to educate and enthrall guests of all ages. Many events take place in and around (depending on the weather) the base lodges of the Bridger Bowl Ski Area. One favorite activity has participants visit educational stations and check off what they see in a passport book that they then turn in for a prize at the end of the day. Hands-on activities include educational stations, a binocular training session, bear spray simulator, and raptor identification. The Montana Raptor Conservation Center also brings live raptors for a close-up view of them.

15795 Bridger Canyon Rd., 406-586-1518
bridgerraptorfest.com

TIP

Because the presence of dogs can spook the raptors, please leave them at home to prevent any changes in the birds' migration behavior.

DINE AT BODHI FARMS' MONTANA

FARM TO TABLE FOOD FESTIVAL

For an intimate gathering revolving around exceptional food, buy your tickets early to attend the Montana Farm to Table Food Festival at Bodhi Farms, a working permaculture farm and eco-resort outside of Bozeman. Every year in July, they curate exceptional chefs to showcase local foods and forward-thinking regional producers. Basking in the joy of the height of the summer under outdoor canopies, guests enjoy live music and the pastoral backdrop of this beautiful farm with stunning views of the Gallatin mountains. It is an opportune time to sample the specialties of these exceptional chefs working with foods at the height of freshness and quality. With a sustainable agricultural model, taking care of the land results in incredible produce that takes center stage at the Montana Farm to Table Food Festival.

13624 S Cottonwood Rd.
bodhi-farms.com

TIP

Even if you cannot attend Bodhi Farms' Farm to Table Food Festival, you can join them for their Thursday evening Farm Parties or Sunday Brunch, both of which feature live music.

MORE CHANCES TO ENJOY EXCELLENT FOOD, DRINK, AND MUSIC

Savor Big Sky

Savor Big Sky kicks off the summer season at the end of June by bringing together regionally inspired food, wine, and music with the scenic splendor at Big Sky Resort. Where else can you have brunch at Mountain Village, then hike (or take the chairlift) to 8,800 feet and toast with one of 200 varieties of wines, ciders, spirits, or handcrafted beers.

50 Big Sky Resort Rd., 800-548-4486
bigskyresort.com/savor

Sweet Pea Festival

If you're in Bozeman during the first weekend of August, do not miss the Sweet Pea Festival, one of Montana's longest-running art festivals, where you'll find visual and musical art as well as theatrical and dance productions.

406-586-4003
sweetpeafestival.org

Summer SLAM Festival

Held in Bogert Park during the first weekend of August, the Summer SLAM Festival showcases dozens of Montana artists and performers, along with offerings for kids.

S Church Ave. and Bogert Pl.
slamfestivals.org

Wildlands Festival

The Wildlands Festival, held at the outdoor Big Sky Arena, is a celebration of music and conservation with the first weekend in August kicking off with a dinner and auction on Thursday evening, followed by two nights of outstanding live performances.

406-995-2055
wildlandsfestival.com

EXPLORE A WIDE VARIETY OF ENTERTAINMENT

AT THE WARREN MILLER PERFORMING ARTS CENTER

The Warren Miller Performing Arts Center (WMPAC) brings in high-level performances you'd expect to find in much larger venues. Seating 280 delighted audience members, this comfortable and visually impactful theater offers an exceptional view of the stage, featuring talent ranging from Losers Cirque, a combination of acrobatics, dance, and live music, to classically trained musicians creating unique soundtracks for classical films. Named after Warren Miller, a beloved local character known for his iconic outdoor adventure films and community support, WMPAC honors his vision by collaborating with the Big Sky community where it offers a home stage for Big Sky Broadway and Big Sky Community Theater, along with theatrical space for Ophir and Lone Peak High School students. Their fall and winter seasons showcase their wide range of theater and dance performances, and the summer is the time for their acoustic musical offerings.

45465 Gallatin Rd., 406-995-6345
(on the campus of Lone Peak High School in Big Sky)
warrenmillerpac.org

GATHER WITH YOUR FRIENDS
AT MUSIC IN THE MOUNTAINS

Meet a couple hundred of your new best friends at Music in the Mountains in Big Sky every Thursday evening from June to September. Top-notch music of all styles, fabulous food, generous drinks, and an outstanding venue at Center State at Len Hill Park in the Big Sky Town Center is the perfect recipe to make strangers feel like family. Music in the Mountains is the ultimate summertime party atmosphere, with the kids playing in the nearby park while zydeco, bomba, Texas blues, metal, rock, and country music echo throughout the valley. Sponsored by the Arts Council of Big Sky, Music in the Mountains supports newer musicians in the Emerging Artists Series to provide an opportunity for attendees to experience a deep pool of talent. The event is free of charge and a perfect way to make every week memorable throughout the summer.

285 Simkins Dr.
bigskyarts.org

TICKLE YOUR FUNNY BONE
AT LAST BEST COMEDY

If laughter is the best medicine, Last Best Comedy is the place for a healthy dose. Currently, Last Best Comedy is the only dedicated comedy club in Montana, and it brings together a wide range of acts to tickle anyone's funny bone. Featuring improv and stand-up, they're open Tuesday through Saturday nights and offer the mic to burgeoning local comedians during the weekday evenings. Because comedy is for everyone, Last Best Comedy provides many classes, including Kid Comedy Camp, where youngsters build their improv skills and gain confidence in front of an audience. Not to ignore the grown-ups, experienced and talented instructors lead students into the world of stand-up and improv. To wrap up the summer, don't miss the Last Best Comedy Festival held in September, where national headliners, such as Montana's very own Reggie Watts, open up the event, inviting performers from throughout the country to shine for three days. With the entrance in the alley, they invite folks to "Come, have a drink, and laugh at stuff."

321 E Main St., 406-219-3393
lastbestcomedy.com

LISTEN TO YOUR FAVORITE MUSIC WITH LOGJAM PRESENTS

With country, rock, metal, and cutting-edge performers, Logjam Presents brings big performances to Bozeman at the historic Rialto and the brand-new Elm. Constructed in 1908, the downtown Rialto began as a storefront and post office for the burgeoning town until the building became a theater in 1924 at the height of the roaring 1920s. After many seasons of engagement and prolonged periods of closure, the restored Rialto has a vibrant new life as a hopping venue for performers in an intimate setting. The Elm is the newest concert venue in Montana, and Logjam Presents rocks the house with its cutting-edge sound system. With a capacity of up to 1,100 people, whether on the tiered main floor or the balcony, every spot provides terrific views of the talent. There is an outdoor patio on the second floor next to the bar, or you can grab a refreshment at the second bar on the first floor.

The Rialto
10 W Main St.
logjampresents.com

The Elm
506 N 7th Ave.

33

FIND YOUR HOLIDAY SPIRIT
AT THE CHRISTMAS STROLL

Santa Claus kicks off the Christmas season with a parade and the ceremonial lighting of the Christmas "spiders" stretching over Main Street. From 4 to 10 p.m. during the first Saturday in December, stroll-goers fill the street from Grand Avenue to Rouse Avenue as holiday music fills the air, dancers entertain the crowds, and organizations offer activities for the entire family, including a climbing wall and an exciting hot-air balloon shooting fire into the sky. Horse-drawn carriage rides add to the holiday ambiance, while marshmallow roasts and photos with Santa at the historic Baxter Hotel, where the event originated decades ago, make the event a memorable Christmas tradition. Shops are open to start checking items off your list, and dozens of fantastic food vendors sell hot, delicious fare. A living nativity scene, complete with animals for the manger, is a sweet reminder of the origin of Christmas. The Christmas Stroll is the perfect time to grab a cup of cocoa or a festive adult beverage and welcome the Christmas season.

downtownbozeman.org

HOLIDAY ACTIVITIES

Belgrade Christmas Convoy

If you want to extend the festivities, be sure to attend the Belgrade Christmas Convoy, which takes place the second weekend of December. Hundreds of decorated trucks and tractors make their way through Belgrade to kick off the holiday season.

mtconvoyfoundation.com

Bozeman Ice Festival

Learn the difference between an A-grade and traverse, along with the nuts and bolts of gear, techniques, and safety at the Bozeman Ice Festival, held each year during the second week of December.

bozemanicefest.com

CATCH UP WITH FRIENDS
AT THE WEEKLY BOZEMAN ART WALKS

The best way to experience Bozeman's thriving art scene is to participate in the Bozeman Art Walks held on the second Friday of each month from June to September from 6 to 8 p.m. The entire downtown area has the celebration vibe; there's line dancing in one of the galleries, comedy acts, a cappella choirs, rock bands, bluegrass music, and other exceptional local talent. During the event, fine artists of all mediums take center stage at local galleries and shops, although the event is not only for art galleries. More than 40 businesses—including ones on the upper levels of the downtown buildings—welcome walk-goers with refreshments and the enthusiasm we all share during these glorious Bozeman summer evenings. The Bozeman Art Walks engage and support local artists. There is also another opportunity to get together during the special Winter Art Walk in early December. Like in the summer, businesses remain open, offering warm refreshments instead of cold lemonade on a winter evening for this festive event to kick off the holiday season.

406-586-4008
downtownbozeman.org

SHAKE YOUR THING
AT MUSIC ON MAIN

With palatable excitement, everyone shares the midsummer energy during Music on Main, a six-week concert series celebrating our brief yet beautiful weather, community togetherness, and exceptional music. Located in historic downtown Bozeman, the road is closed to traffic along Main Street from Rouse Avenue to Black Avenue from 6:30 to 8:30 p.m. on Thursday evenings from mid-July through mid-August. Music on Main is a good example of a way Bozeman remains a typical Montana small town, as this enthusiastic gathering brings together Bozmanites and visitors alike to listen to talented musicians, meet new friends, shop at local stores that remain open late, and enjoy fabulous food and drinks. With at least 18 food trucks offering Lebanese, Mexican, great curries, good old-fashioned American hot dogs, and much more, they feed around 6,000 people every week, making this a highlight of the summer for a lot of the community.

downtownbozeman.org

TIP

There's no need to leave the kids at home while you chat with friends. The Lehrkinds Coca-Cola Kids' Zone on South Bozeman Avenue offers inflatable jump houses and other activities provided by local nonprofit organizations to keep the kids entertained.

GET LOST
IN THE MONTANA CORN MAZE

Grown on a third-generation family farm originally homesteaded in 1897 and now stewarded by Rose (Bos) and her husband, John Brouwer, the Montana Corn Maze is a favorite autumn tradition. Sixteen miles west of town, the six-acre corn maze takes center stage each year, showcasing a new design like the MSU Bobcats or Bighole Battlefield, all carefully cut using GPS guidance when the corn is a mere six inches tall in the spring. Guests jump aboard the wagon to reach the corn patch, enjoying beautiful views of the surrounding mountains as they roll to the maze. There are challenges for all ages and skill levels, so everyone has a good time finding their way among the tall corn stalks. Spend the entire day here with trikes for the kids (and grown-up kids) to ride, disc golf, miniature golf, cornhole, a bale pyramid, a playground, a sandbox, and a wagon depot slide. Several exceptional local food trucks are also on-site. Hang out, have a picnic, and enjoy one of the most beautiful times of the year.

4605 W Cameron Bridge Rd., 406-922-1643
montanacornmaze.com

TIP

This is a terrific place to pick up your fall pumpkins and fresh flowers for as long as they last into the season.

HEAR THE JOY
WITH BAROQUE MUSIC MONTANA

Music tells a story, and the baroque musical style purports life as theater while giving us a glimpse of the dazzling machinations of the world's power players behind the scenes. These timeless tales illuminate humanity's extravagance and expressive nature in this post-Renaissance era when significant social change reshaped European culture circa 1600–1750. Familiar baroque composers, such as Handel, Vivaldi, and Bach, created this style, often for kings and royalty, developing unique elements within their music. Baroque Music Montana (BaMM) delights modern audiences through regular performances in the Bozeman area, offering a fresh exploration of these classic elements of love, political drama, and human nature, and coordinating with the talent of internationally known classical singers, including members of Opera Montana. BaMM is also an educational touchstone for musical artists throughout the entire Northwest, offering workshops and opportunities to people of all ages.

406-599-3397
baroquemusicmontana.com

TIP

Keep an eye out for Bach on the Trail, where musicians perform at several trailheads around Bozeman, bringing this rich musical tradition to the beautiful landscape, much to the joy of all trail users.

SPIN YOUR WAY ONTO THE DANCE FLOOR

WITH WESTERN ROOTS COUNTRY DANCING

Even if you don't know the difference between two-step and country swing, Western Roots Country Dancing will give you all the moves you need to show your stuff on the dance floor. This enthusiastic crew offers group lessons throughout the week ranging from linedancing to basic country steps to intermediate country swing moves. They also offer private lessons to sharpen your dance skills! Their experienced instructors can sort out even those who have never danced in their lives. The whole reason to learn what to do on the dance floor is to have fun, so you want to make a night of it with friends. RSVP to one of their many group events to ensure a memorable night out. Western Roots Country Dancing hosts a dance competition at the Big Sky Country State Fair for the perfect opportunity to show off your skills.

58 Silver Leaf Ln., 406-570-7422
mtcountrydance.com

TIP

Kick up your heels at the Jump in Gallatin Gateway, Tips Up in Big Sky, or Willie's Distillery in Ennis. Western Roots offers somewhere to dance nearly every day of the week.

GET A LITTLE WESTERN
AT THE ROCKING R BAR

The Rocking R has been a fixture in Bozeman since 1947 as the gathering spot for locals and students in the heart of downtown. Fifty-four years after its creation, the R Bar got a new look with a complete remodel, although it was short-lived when a gas explosion destroyed the entire block in 2009. By 2011, the Rocking R was back, better than ever, with its enormous dance floor and outdoor patio area for people to gather during the summer. It doesn't matter what day it is; there is always something happening at the Rocking R. Throughout the week, bingo, trivia, and karaoke are always a good way to relax and have fun with friends. In the middle of the week, "Wild West Wednesdays" feature a DJ playing requests, dancing until midnight, and sometimes, the mechanical bull available to take on all brave riders. The weekends are hopping with more dancing, music, and special events throughout the year, and it makes sense that this is a favorite hangout for students and locals alike.

211 E Main St., 406-587-9355
rockingrbar.com

TIP

During football season, Bobcat fans head to the Rocking R for the "Fifth Quarter" after every game for discounted beers and commemorative glasses.

Climbing at Spire

SPORTS AND RECREATION

CLIMB THE WALLS
AT SPIRE CLIMBING + FITNESS

Hone your climbing skills at Spire Climbing + Fitness, the 17,000-square-foot indoor climbing facility where novice and experienced climbers alike challenge themselves and improve their abilities. For those new to the sport, the auto-belay stations offer security while climbing the 50-foot-high walls. It's an adrenaline rush as you push back from the wall and gracefully float to the floor! Instructors give participants a lesson on the equipment and points on safety. After a test fall, climbers are free to head for the ceiling. Experienced climbers tackle the top-rope climbs with a belay partner, and for bouldering enthusiasts, straight runs and overhangs offer problems ranging from V-0 to the expert level V-12s. Spire offers classes and one-on-one instruction. The fitness area provides equipment and classes to strengthen your body for the sport. Climbing-specific gear, such as hang boards, a system wall, a campus board, weight vests, and pulley systems, are also available for more focused training.

13 Enterprise Blvd., 406-586-0706
spireclimbing.com

TIP

Spire also has a 2,600-square-foot bouldering and fitness training area on the west side of Bozeman at 10 Innovation Lane, Unit C. 406-586-2814

CARRY ON THE TRADITION

AND HIKE THE M

Hiking to the 240-foot-high and 100-foot-wide, bright white M is a right of passage for those living and visiting Bozeman. A group of Montana State University engineering students built the eye-catching emblem in 1916 by packing the limestone rocks up the mountain before carefully placing and whitewashing them to create this longstanding symbol of local pride. Since then, the trails to and around the M have beckoned hikers, trail runners, dog walkers, and mountain bikers. Take the trail to the right if you want a quick way to elevate your heart rate, or follow the path on the left for a more leisurely route. Take your time to enjoy the wilderness or spectacular views of the Gallatin Valley, or for a longer day head to the top of Big Baldy and the Bridger Foothills Trail #534, which travels 20 miles to Fairy Lake.

Bridger Canyon Rd.
406-587-8404

TIP

The southern exposure of the M Trail makes it a favorite on chilly days during the winter, but it is open and hot on summer afternoons. Hike early when it's warm, and bring water, even for a short outing.

FLOAT ABOVE THE VALLEY
WITH ENDEAVOR BALLOONING

Experience a bird's-eye view of the Gallatin Valley's winding rivers, green fields, and splendid mountains by hopping and taking a hot-air balloon ride with Endeavor Ballooning. The approximately one-hour flight takes you between 200 and 2,500 feet above the landscape, and the one-of-a-kind experience gives passengers a panoramic view as they glide quietly over stunningly beautiful country. Senior pilot and co-owner, Colin Graham, has been a mountain pilot all his adult life. He fell in love with hot-air ballooning at his year-round home in the Gallatin Valley. His enthusiasm is contagious as passengers prepare for their ride with his experienced crew, who take care of everything, including taking you to the launch site and retrieving you when you land. Expect mimosas or champagne as a celebratory beverage at the end of your memorable float over the valley!

406-600-8999
montanaballoon.com

TIP

Endeavor Ballooning offers flights in Bozeman and Big Sky to accommodate your preference.

TAKE THE LIFT AND RIDE YOUR MOUNTAIN BIKE

AT BIG SKY RESORT

When the snow is gone and the wildflowers are blooming, it's time to bike the trails at Big Sky Resort. Clip your bike into the bike lift while you ride up comfortably on their highly advanced chairlifts—the Ramcharger 8, Swift Current 6, or Explorer 2—that offer inspiring scenic rides. At the top, enjoy the spectacular views, take a deep breath, and head down the well-constructed trails that meet all skill—and thrill—levels. More accessible flow trails like Snake Charmer and Gambler feature smoother runs, while Soul Hole is bound to offer a gripping challenge. There are bike rentals and knowledgeable guides available to show you the terrain. Big Sky Resort offers private and group lessons for new bikers or those who want to work on their skills, including a women's biking series and kids' camps.

50 Big Sky Resort Rd., 800-548-4486
bigskyresort.com

TIP

Besides the buzz of activity with mountain bikers during the summer, Big Sky Resort has equally remarkable hiking trails. Take advantage of one of the guided hikes to learn about the remarkable flora and fauna while enjoying this tranquil time on the mountain.

PADDLE YOUR FAVORITE CRAFT
ON HYALITE RESERVOIR

Gliding along the calm water of Hyalite Reservoir first thing in the morning, you're surrounded by dense forests and towering ridges, making it feel like you're deep within the wilderness instead of 30 minutes from town. You can launch boats from Hood Creek Campground or the day-use area at the north end of the lake. Stand up paddle boards (SUPs) and kayaks are two of the most popular ways to make the most of a warm day. Canoes, sailboats, tubes, rowboats, and even powerboats with low-speed trolling motors are welcome on the 206-acre lake. There is a no-wake policy on the water to keep activity calm and enjoyable for everyone. Hyalite is one of the most popular recreational areas around Bozeman, but if you venture onto the water early in the morning or during the weekday, you're more likely to have a relaxing, more intimate experience.

Hyalite Canyon Rd., 406-522-2520
hyalite.org

TIP

For kayakers looking for short-but-sweet runs to hone their skills, the class 4 boulder rapids along Hyalite Creek are a terrific spot for a quick outing.

SADDLE UP
AT MEDICINE LAKE OUTFITTERS

Swing into the saddle at Medicine Lake Outfitters for a two-hour ride along bridle paths that wind through shaded cottonwood stands and wildflower-filled openings along Baker Creek on gentle horses. Soak in the spectacular views of the Bridger Range and the Spanish Peaks as your guide leads the way during this peaceful walk where you might catch a glimpse of bald eagles, sandhill cranes, wild turkeys, and even an industrious beaver as your horse follows the path. The knowledgeable crew at Medicine Lake Outfitters matches riders with the best horse for their skill level and gives everyone a primer on horse etiquette and trail safety to ensure a pleasant ride for all. Those who wish for an extended outing have options of all-day excursions in the Madison and Bridger Ranges or exploring the west side of Yellowstone National Park for a memorable Montana adventure.

346 Linney Spur Rd., 406-388-4938
bozeman-horseback-riding.com

TIP

Be sure to make your reservation online before visiting the ranch, and even though Medicine Lake Outfitters is only 15 minutes outside of town, the GPS directions can be tricky. It is best to follow the directions on their website.

CRUISE FROM MAIN STREET
TO THE MOUNTAINS

One of the most incredible aspects of Bozeman is that the outdoor recreational opportunities are practically out your back door. These trails and natural areas include several exceptional and accessible bicycling routes, totaling roughly 90 miles, that take you from Main Street to the surrounding foothills. One of the longer connected routes begins near the Bozeman Public Library at Lindley Park and cruises through residential areas to Highland Glen Nature Preserve, a cooperative effort between Bozeman Health, the Gallatin Valley Land Trust, and other local entities. A series of single tracks courses through the rolling hills, grasslands, aspen groves, deep gullies, and wetlands of this natural area, all surrounded by beautiful views of the Bridger Mountains. Highland Glen can be biked as a single loop or connected to the Painted Hills Trail system on Kagy Boulevard.

406-587-8404
gvlt.org

TIP

To have an overview of the exceptional Gallatin Valley Land Trust trails and natural areas on hand, pick up one of their maps at local stores or through their website.

OUTWIT A TROUT
WITH THE RIVER'S EDGE

Standing waist-deep in a river, cold water swirling around you as you read the swirls and eddies that might hide a wily trout, is quintessentially Montanan. The excitement of the fish grabbing the carefully presented fly and dashing off is the only thing that breaks your peace. If you're going to learn to fly-fish with confidence that leads you to these famous Montana waters, spend time with the best at the River's Edge. Their fly-fishing classes teach you to get into a fish's mind, figure out its behavior, and discover what it means to "match the hatch" to choose the right fly. These small classes with one to four students last three hours and provide lots of one-on-one time with experienced instructors happy to take you through every step, from learning how to tie a proper knot to reading the water to expertly releasing a fish. They also offer advanced classes to learn new techniques or troubleshoot any issues you feel you have.

59 North Star Ln., 406-284-2401
theriversedgewest.com

TIP

Once you're ready to venture to the streams and rivers, sign up for a guided trip with the River's Edge folks for time at premier fishing areas.

DISCOVER NEW AREAS
WITH WILD MONTANA

One of the best ways to explore the practically unlimited hiking opportunities is with the knowledgeable and enthusiastic leaders of Wild Montana's Madison–Gallatin Chapter. This nonprofit organization hosts summer and winter walks led by locals passionate about the area. Walks vary each season, but one of the favorites is Cowboy Heaven on the west side of the Madison Range. This six-mile round-trip hike features flower-filled open meadows and deep forests with views of the Lee Metcalf Wilderness. Another is to Windy Pass Cabin, located on the Gallatin Crest with an elevation of around 10,000 feet and one of the wildest places in the Lower 48. Even in the winter, join them on Winter Walks to snowshoe into places such as Porcupine Creek or Lava Lake. All of their outings are excellent opportunities to learn more about the area with like-minded folk.

wildmontana.org

TIP

This welcoming group loves to share their knowledge of the natural world. Come with your questions about flowers, geography, wildlife, or what to pack on hikes.

CHEER
FOR THE BOBCATS!

The crisp fall air and students returning to classes at Montana State University mean only one thing: It's Bobcat season in Bozeman. Roaring with more than 17,000 enthusiastic fans, home game weekends at Bobcat Stadium are a raucous good time as locals, alums, and eager visitors come together to cheer on their favorite football team. With a program beginning in 1897, the Bobcats often dominate the Big Sky Conference in the NCAA's Division 1 Football Championship Subdivision, and have bragging rights from three national championships. There's particular excitement when the Bobcats play their rival, the University of Montana Grizzlies, in the annual Cat–Griz game, also known as the Brawl of the Wild. Tailgating is as traditional as cheering for the team. The parking lots surrounding Bobcat Stadium and the south lot of Brick Breeden Fieldhouse are designated pregame celebrations where you can grill brats and enjoy a few beverages.

406-994-5694
msubobcats.com

TIP

The games in October and November have a reputation for being chilly, or downright cold, so dress accordingly. Wear layers of clothing, including lighter base layers for the afternoons when the sun comes out, and bring a heavy winter coat for those autumn storms.

SOAK AWAY YOUR CARES
AT BOZEMAN HOT SPRINGS

Soaking in these warm, mineral-rich waters calms the machinations of your mind and relaxes your body, particularly after taking advantage of all of the exceptional outdoor experiences around Bozeman. Fortunately, this region, born of volcanic activity, is a hot spot for hot springs.

Eight miles west of town, Bozeman Hot Springs has welcomed guests since 1879, when Jeremiah Mathews built private bathing rooms and a 14-by-18-foot pool to accommodate travelers. Newly renovated, Bozeman Hot Springs features eight interior pools, including two cold plunges for hearty souls, along with four beautifully landscaped outdoor pools. Each of the pools on the inside and outside has a different temperature for you to find that perfect level of heat. There is live music on the outdoor stage on Thursday and Sunday evenings during the summer, which makes for a perfect wrap-up of the day. Bozeman Hot Springs are open year round, and it's particularly magical when your hair is frozen yet you are still toasty warm in the pool.

81123 Gallatin Rd., 406-586-6492
bozemanhotsprings.co

TIP

Bozeman Hot Springs pools, gym, and spa are closed from sundown on Friday to sundown on Saturday, so plan accordingly.

SEARCH OUT MORE HOT SPRINGS

Norris Hot Springs

Thirty-six miles west of Bozeman, Norris Hot Springs has a fun and funky vibe where the endless blue sky or expanse of stars is your ceiling over the outdoor pool. Live music happens in the geodesic dome, and they offer fresh, organic food, much of it grown in their geothermally heated greenhouse.

42 MT-84, Norris, 406-685-3303
norrishotsprings.com

Chico Hot Springs

Located 48 miles away in the tiny town of Pray, the historic resort is replete with reported ghosts and a high-quality restaurant. Established in 1900, the outfit catered to gold miners, and over a century later, visitors enjoy the actual treasure: two sparkling outdoor pools to soak in at any time of the year.

163 Chico Rd., 406-333-4933
chicohotsprings.com

EXPLORE
MAJESTIC OUSEL FALLS

Hiking to a waterfall is like finding the end of a beautiful rainbow, and Ousel Falls is especially magical because it is easy to reach. The trailhead is located two miles southwest of Big Sky along Highway 191. The large parking area with a restroom facility and information board tends to fill up early on the weekends, although evening strolls are often a good time to visit. The round-trip hike is less than two miles long along a wide, gradually sloping path, mainly through the trees, with 242 feet in elevation change. A wide wooden bridge crosses the South Fork West Fork Gallatin River, which is a good place to try your hand at fly-fishing at some of the calmer pools. Courteous dogs, or those on leashes, are welcome on the trail. After the ups and downs of the terrain to reach the falls, there is a lovely viewing platform above the wide, beautiful falls, making it a terrific place for a picnic.

Ousel Falls Rd., 406-993-2112
outsidebozeman.com/places/trails/ousel-falls-park-trail

CONTINUE ON A FULL-FLEDGED WATERFALL TOUR

Pioneer Falls

Starting at the Spanish Creek Campground, this six-mile hike with 800 feet of elevation gain pays off with the stunning 40-foot cascading falls.

Spanish Creek Campground
outsidebozeman.com/trails-tours/hiking-trails/pioneer-falls

Palisade Falls

Found near Hyalite Reservoir, a mile-long paved trail climbs 250 feet to these dramatic falls. Go before 9 a.m. or on a weekday to have the falls primarily to yourself.

FS 3165, 406-522-2520
visitmt.com/listings/general/national-forest-trail/palisade-falls-trail

Grotto Falls

Located near Hyalite Reservoir, the packed-gravel trail through mature conifer forests and flower-filled meadows is family friendly and accommodates strollers and wheelchairs.

406-522-2520
visitmt.com/listings/general/national-forest-trail/grotto-falls

Champagne Falls

Along the Hyalite Creek Trail, the hike to Champagne Falls climbs 1,240 feet in elevation to see the twisting falls spilling over the rocks.

406-522-2520

Tip: Many of these waterfalls are popular destinations in the winter. Strap on snowshoes and check them out in their frozen finery.

MUSH A DOGSLED
WITH MORRISON RACING KENNEL

Dash through the snow with a team of sled dogs with Morrison Racing Kennel. The huskies' sheer joy and excitement in doing what they are born to do travels through the lines, making this an exhilarating experience whether you're driving the team or going along for the ride. Double-driver sleds offer guests the chance to stand behind the team and drive the sled with the guidance of an experienced musher. For those who would rather sit back and enjoy the beautiful scenery, the toboggan provides a comfortable seat, especially for parents with younger children, to soak in the experience. During this 10-mile round trip, the teams travel trails in the Mill Creek area, approximately 15 minutes from Pray, and stop at scenic points to marvel at the mountain views. The dogs love attention, and guests are encouraged to be generous with their affection to praise these friendly, furry athletes.

406-270-6948
morrisonracingkennel.com

TIP

The dogs are happiest when it's cold, and the tours run in temperatures as cold as -20 Fahrenheit. To remain warm, especially when you're not moving, dress in layers and bring your hat and gloves.

HOLD A POSE
AT YOGA FOR ALL AT THE BOZEMAN PUBLIC LIBRARY

A good day is only made better by joining the free, hour-long yoga class for all at the Bozeman Public Library. Held every Tuesday at 12:15 p.m., you don't even have to change out of your jeans to follow their certified instructor through a gentle flow series suitable for all skill levels. Bring your mat (or borrow one in a pinch) and find your space on the lawn at Lindley Park, close to the fairy garden in the northwest corner, during the summer. Children are welcome, and it's common for babies to hang out near Mom (or Dad), plus have the older kids play or join along during this rejuvenating workout. As the weather cools, the group meets in the large common room inside the library, yet the enthusiasm never dampens regardless of the weather. Check out the library for other offerings, such as gyrokinesis, qigong, and walking groups.

626 E Main St., 406-582-2400
bozemanlibrary.org

TIP

Also check out the Belgrade Community Library as they offer a number of free fitness classes throughout the year.

106 N Broadway Ave., 406-388-4346
belgradelibrary.org

SHRED THE GNAR
AT BIG SKY RESORT

With more than 300 runs offering 4,350 vertical feet over the resort's 5,850 acres, everything is big at Big Sky Resort. Located only 50 miles south of Bozeman, there are unlimited possibilities for visitors and locals alike. The technological marvels of their chairlift systems bring skiers complete comfort; several of the lifts feature ergonomic, heated seats, and a Big Sky Blue Bubble to protect riders from inclement weather. Even the surface lifts are encased in a protective cover to make traveling between runs pleasant. Try headlamp night skiing or take the entire family to the Enchanted Forest, which is lit with more than 10,000 lights dangling from the trees and illuminating a kilometer path through the forest, and then wrap up the experience at an outdoor fire. Even if you are not skiing, make a reservation at Everett's 8800 to enjoy an exceptional dining experience atop Andesite Mountain.

50 Big Sky Resort Rd., 800-548-4486
bigskyresort.com

TIP

For a truly unforgettable Montana experience, take the Lone Peak Tram to the top of Lone Peak at Big Sky Resort. Whether you visit in the winter or summer, the serene and comfortable journey to the top of the 11,166-foot-high Lone Peak is a breathtaking and awe-inspiring experience that will leave you speechless.

SKI CLOSE TO TOWN AT BRIDGER BOWL

A local favorite, Bridger Bowl is 16 miles out of Bozeman and offers more than 75 marked runs (with many unmarked routes) over 2,000 acres. Eight chairlifts take skiers to a maximum height of 8,700 feet. And with an average of 300 inches of snow each winter, their season, running from mid-December through mid-April, is a thrill. Jim Bridger and Saddle Peak Lodges handle many guest services, offering meals and drinks, and Deer Park Chalet and Alpine Cabin provide food and beverages to famished skiers.

15795 Bridger Canyon Rd., 406-587-2111
bridgerbowl.com

55

GLIDE THROUGH A WINTER WONDERLAND
IN HYALITE CANYON

When winter snows blanket the valley, Hyalite Canyon is the hot spot for cross-country skiers and snowshoers to explore more than 18 miles of groomed trails and nearly limitless backcountry options. Hyalite Canyon Road is plowed to Hyalite Reservoir, the starting point to a wide choice of trails of varying difficulty levels. Park at the Hyalite Reservoir day-use area, Lick Creek, History Rock, Chisolm, or the Grotto Falls trailhead to start your journey. Skiers looking for a shorter, more accessible route should consider the Westshore Trail, which travels through meadows and snow-covered forests for 1.2 miles to the Crescent Lake Junction. For a more challenging outing, jump off at Lick Creek, which gains enough elevation to offer spectacular views of the reservoir and Hyalite Peaks. The reservoir's west side receives less sun, so it typically has deeper, fluffier snow conditions, and the 10-mile trip around the reservoir is a favorite for many Nordic skiers.

hyalite.org

MORE TRAILS CLOSE TO TOWN

The Bridger Ski Foundation manages exceptional Nordic skiing and snowshoe trails to make winter recreation accessible to everyone.

Highland Glen Nature Preserve

To ski the six miles of rolling, open terrain with a few steeper hills for a little extra excitement, park at the Softball Complex lot on the corner of Ellis Street and Highland Boulevard. It is also possible to connect from Highland Glen to the more advanced Kagy Loop and add additional miles.

Sunset Hills

This three-mile loop starts at the same parking area at the Softball Complex, but is located north of Highland Glen between there and Lindley Park. This is mainly gentle terrain that is ideal for beginners. The Bridger Ski Foundation makes snow when necessary.

Bozeman Creek/Sourdough Canyon

The main parking area is at the end of Sourdough Canyon Road, and the wide, groomed trail follows Bozeman Creek through Forest Service Land. For an extended day, you can continue another 10 miles (one-way) to reach Mystic Lake, a popular area for winter enthusiasts.

Bridger Creek Golf Course

Begin at the clubhouse and ski either loop—or do both to total up to five miles of easy, rolling terrain. Dogs are not allowed on this route.

Chief Joseph Middle School

Chief Joseph is another convenient and beginner-friendly route. It is a three-quarters-mile loop around the middle school's fields, which are available when school is not in session.

406-587-2445
bridgerskifoundation.org/trails/maps

GO WITH THE FLOW
WITH MADISON RIVER TUBING

Floating the Madison River with Madison River Tubing is the best way to beat the heat on hot summer days. They provide cloth-covered, vinyl-free tubes with mesh bottoms so your own bottom doesn't fall through, and the tubes can connect to float as a group. This gentle stretch of the river averages between six inches to five feet deep, making it suitable for kids as young as 3. It requires between 1.5 and 2.5 hours to float for a short, relaxing experience. Besides the tubes and optional stand-up paddle boards (SUPs), Madison River Tubing provides life jackets for all participants. You can even rent a cooler tube with ice to keep your cold beverages with you. Bring (or rent) a waterproof camera case so you can take photos along the way. To reach the river, meet at the specified access site or have them shuttle you from Bozeman. Either way, they'll pick you up at the end of your trip and bring you back to where you need to be.

1110 W Main St., 406-209-8384
madisonrivertubing.com

TIP

For an adrenaline-surging river outing, Madison River Tubing also offers whitewater rafting trips through Beartrap Canyon, a beautiful stretch of the river that flows past towering cliffs and provides opportunities to view eagles and other wildlife.

SOAR THROUGH THE TREES ON A ZIP LINE
AT MONTANA WHITEWATER

You'll fly over the river and through the woods zip-lining with Montana Whitewater in Gallatin Gateway, roughly 15 miles from Bozeman. To begin your adrenaline-spiking adventure, their safety-minded crew shows you the ropes. They educate you on the proper form and fit for the harness before sending you to climb the forest bridges to the platforms standing over 50 feet high. Different routes, such as the Wiley Wire of the Wild West, send you flying 800 feet across the Gallatin River at 40 miles per hour. Or head to Grandma's House, where you cross the river and zip over the trees. Besides the exciting zip-line features, the canopy walks are heart-pounding thrills, including Bill's Revenge, where you step from one swaying swing to another before climbing into a massive cargo net. Private tours are also available.

63960 Gallatin Rd., 406-763-4465
montanawhitewater.com

TIP

Montana Whitewater also offers rafting trips in the Yellowstone, Madison, and Gallatin Rivers, along with tube floats down the Madison.

CHILL OUT
AT GALLATIN ICE

Gallatin Ice is the hot spot for winter sports, offering a place to skate and watch sporting events, including hockey, figure skating, and curling in their two separate buildings at the Gallatin County Fairgrounds. Partake in open skate, or take lessons with their world-class instructors. Gallatin Ice is where you hone your hockey skating skills or become part of the hockey scene. Join Puck Lunch, the Monday-to-Friday pickup game that welcomes adults from 11 a.m. to 12:50 p.m., or become part of one of the dozens of hockey teams. For new players, the Hoctober Scramble is a short season that runs from September to October and makes for a good initiation, but once you're hooked, there are multiple adult hockey leagues, including the Women's Weasel League. If you'd rather watch a game, their season is packed from September to March—and beyond, for playoffs. During the winter, catch the NA3HL Ice Dogs or Montana State University hockey games.

901 N Black Ave., 406-586-5557
gallatinice.org

TIP

If you're looking for outdoor ice, there are several city parks available when the winter weather cooperates.

Southside Park, 411 W College St. Beall Park, 415 N Bozeman Ave.

Anderson Pavilion at Bogert Park, 325 S Church Ave.

TAKE YOUR DOG FOR A WALK
AT SNOWFILL RECREATION AREA

Snowfill is one of the most beautiful dog parks you'll ever see, particularly in the spring and early summer when the green rolling hills are an eye-catching contrast against the mountain backdrop. Surprisingly, this is a former site of a city landfill. Yet, a cooperative effort between the Gallatin Valley Land Trust, the City of Bozeman, and multiple local businesses transformed the 37 acres into premier fenced off-leash parks where dogs of all sizes can run until their hearts are content. With two miles of gravel trails that stay relatively mud-free even in the rainy season, it's also a terrific place to stretch our legs while taking in the stunning views of the Gallatin Valley and Bridger Mountains. There is a water pump to refresh your furry companions after their run, a dog waste station so you don't have to take your poo bag home, as well as a vault toilet for humans.

Gallatin Valley Land Trust
406-587-8404
gvlt.org

WHOOP IT UP
AT THE BOZEMAN STAMPEDE

From the earliest cowboying days, ranch hands tested their skills against their stock and each other, showing off who could stay on the most untamed bronc the longest or wrestle a steer (also called bulldogging) to the ground the fastest. By the 1880s, these events grew in popularity at venues such as Buffalo Bill's Wild West Show, leading to the highly popular sport today, and multiple events in the Bozeman area carry on this tradition. The Bozeman Stampede is a three-day PRCA event held in August at the Gallatin County Fairgrounds. You'll be able to cheer for your favorite animal and human athletes in saddle bronc, bareback, bull riding, steer wrestling, tie-down roping, team roping, barrel racing, and breakaway roping—along with fun events such as the kids' mutton busting and the downright insane bull scramble, where folks in a bubble suit dodge a bull.

901 N Black Ave.,
bozemanstampede.com

MORE RODEOS IN THE AREA

Valley View Rodeo Series

Valley View Rodeo Series is a summertime favorite, offering nearly weekly contests through June, July, and August. In addition to the standard stock and timed events, they include junior steer riding and junior barrels for young competitors.

901 N Black Ave., 406-285-4411
valleyviewrodeo.com

Bozeman Ranch Rodeo

For a different twist, check out the Bozeman Ranch Rodeo Roundup at the Gallatin County Fairgrounds, which features wild cow milking, team sorting, ranch bronc riding, team doctoring, trailer loading, the hide race, and team branding.

gallatincountyfairgrounds.com

NRA Three Forks Rodeo

Every July, plan to attend the annual National Rodeo Association Three Forks Rodeo and Rodeo Dayz. Expect to watch classic rodeo events, plus kids' events and a popular street dance.

5691 MT-2, 406-272-3716
threeforksrodeo.com

Big Sky PBR

Watch the best bull riders in the world at the Big Sky Professional Bull Riders during this weekend-long event at the Big Sky Event Arena. These hardcore athletes—the riders and the 2,000-pound bulls—thrill the crowd as riders try to hold on for the longest eight seconds of their lives.

450 Aspen Leaf Dr.
bigskypbr.com

SCREAM FOR YOUR FAVORITE SKATERS

AT GALLATIN ROLLER DERBY

It's all about the jam for the Gallatin Roller Derby skaters in the rough-and-tumble sport of flat-track roller derby. In this high-energy and colorful sport, it's hard to know who to watch as the four blockers on each team plow into the others, trying to make space for their jammers—the ones with the stars on their helmets—to skate through the pack to score points each time they lap the opposing team members. These fierce ladies take on a different persona while on track, earning outlandishly funny derby names and wearing bright uniforms in what some people described as a "mosh pit on wheels." These athletes are far from delicate little flowers concerned about breaking a nail. Instead, they count bruises and rink rashes at the end of the bout, all for the delight of the crowd, who quickly turn into devoted fans cheering on their favorite derby skaters. Make a point to cheer on the wild action of a Gallatin Roller Derby home bout at Haynes Pavilion at the Gallatin Valley Fairgrounds on select dates during the summer.

Haynes Pavilion
901 N Black Ave.
grderby.com

TIP

Gallatin Valley Rollers is always looking for "fresh meat," new players who want to learn the sport. They provide the gear and the training, even if you've never been on skates, so don't hesitate to contact them if you want to be part of this thrilling and intense competition.

Tepee at Headwaters State Park

CULTURE AND HISTORY

DIG UP DIRT ABOUT BOZEMAN
AT THE EXTREME HISTORY PROJECT

History isn't pretty, but it certainly is entertaining, especially when shared by the insightful ladies of the Extreme History Project. Their headquarters on the first floor of a former upscale 1891 brothel are in the heart of one of Bozeman's more colorful historical areas. The jaw-dropping tales of early Bozeman come to life through their research, including the colorful madams who once managed the establishment where their headquarters resides, along with the Chinese community members who traveled to this foreign land in search of gold and a means of survival, carving their place in this rugged land. The Extreme History Project in-house tours illuminate fascinating stories while pointing out curated objects. The highly popular Walking History Tours delight visitors and residents alike during the warmer months. These outings take visitors along the streets of Bozeman, sharing the stories behind the people who built the town and exploring Sunset Hills Cemetery, where Bozeman's most colorful characters now rest.

234 E Mendenhall St., 406-220-2678
extremehistoryproject.org

TIP

When you can't join them on in-person tours, tune in to their *Dirt on the Past* podcast for a deep dive into many Bozeman-centric topics.

LIVE IN THE PAST (AND SEE INTO THE FUTURE) AT THE MUSEUM OF THE ROCKIES

"Big Mike," the Tyrannosaurus, welcomes guests at the entrance of the Museum of the Rockies, the premier dinosaur museum and research facility in the region. With the involvement of Montana State University researchers and the museum's top-notch scientists, the *Dinosaurs Under the Big Sky* exhibit in the Siebel Dinosaur Complex offers the "wow factor" for enthusiasts. Beyond stepping back millions of years, additional exhibits highlight the connection to the land of the Indigenous people and provide glimpses of the early Montana lifestyle. There are examples of homes, items of daily life, and several modes of vehicles, including a carriage from the stagecoach days in Yellowstone National Park. The Museum of the Rockies is not only about the past. Looking up and ahead to the future, the Taylor Planetarium puts us in the front row to witness our remarkable universe during their hourly shows. Sit back in the comfortable seats as the cosmos expands before our eyes and learn about our recent space endeavors and the exciting moments yet to come.

600 W Kagy Blvd., 406-994-2251
museumoftherockies.org

TIP

From mid-May to Labor Day, visit the Tinsley Family Homestead at the adjacent Living History Farm. Enjoy a glimpse of their 1889 lifestyle, explore the home and gardens, and witness some of the day-to-day activities from that era.

EXPERIENCE THE VIBRANCY
OF THE STORY MANSION

Even after a century, the Story Mansion is an impressive testament to the intrepid determination of Montana pioneer and entrepreneur Nelson Story and his family. The mansion was built by T. Byron Story, son of Nelson Story, as a home for his wife, Katheryn Ferris, and his five children in 1910. Costing over $50,0000 to build, the 22-room mansion featured the finest woodwork and locally quarried stone blocks. Starting in 1923, Sigma Alpha Epsilon used it for a fraternity house until 2000. In 2008, Friends of the Story Mansion took the reins, refurbishing the home and opening its doors for everyone. The Story Mansion is open the first Sunday of each month from noon until 2 p.m. Stretch a blanket on the lawn to watch a movie during Story Under the Stars, or celebrate Halloween by trick-or-treating at the grand residence during Witches Night. There are also book signings and speakers, pop-up farmers markets, cabinets of curiosity, and cookie painting get-togethers.

811 S Willson Ave.
friendsofthestory.org

TIP

One of the favorite events is the Victorian Holiday Tea held in December. Guests enjoy hot tea and light refreshments served in elegant china in the holiday-adorned mansion.

ENJOY A CARRIAGE RIDE ALONG THE BON TON HISTORIC HOME DISTRICT WITH SUNRISE PACK STATION

During the summer season, ride in a horse-drawn carriage with the Sunrise Pack Station to explore the Bon Ton Home District. Derived from the French phrase *le bon ton*, meaning "good or elegant form or style," these homes were the outward expression of cultural refinement and the burgeoning progress of the town. Beginning around 1883, when the Northern Pacific Railroad arrived in Bozeman, 260 elegant homes were built on South Willson, South Grand, South Third, and West Cleveland, many of which were designed by the eminent architect Fred F. Willson. To best appreciate these early residences, the McClains of Sunrise Pack Station hitch up their team of distinctive Norwegian fjord horses and wheel along the shaded, tree-lined streets, pointing out the unique architectural features and sharing stories of early Bozeman residents. They offer half-hour and hour-long tours, and the carriage can comfortably carry six people.

406-579-9642
sunrisepackstation.com

TIP

In the fall and winter, Sunrise Pack Station offers hay wagon rides and sleigh rides to soak in the ambiance of the season at their ranch near the East Gallatin River, which is less than five miles outside of town.

TRAVEL ALONG ANCIENT PATHS
AT THE MADISON BUFFALO JUMP STATE PARK

For over 2,000 years, Indigenous people from throughout the region drove herds of bison over the 150-foot-high limestone cliff to harvest the animals for food and tools necessary for their daily lives. A skilled, brave young man, draped with a bison calf hide, served as the "runner," acting like a lost calf to catch the attention of the lead bison cow. As she, and the rest of the herd, investigated, other young men wearing wolf hides ran at the herd, driving them over the edge while the initial runner jumped to a safe area. The rest of the tribe was ready at the base of the cliff to process the dead and dying animals, putting up stores for the season. Today we can find tepee rings at the top of the jump and well-worn paths. There are myriad trails in the peaceful 638-acre state park offering spectacular views of the Madison River Valley.

6990 Buffalo Jump Rd., Three Forks, 406-285-3610
fwp.mt.gov/stateparks/madison-buffalo-jump

TIP

There are few trees along any of the trails, so it is best to hike in the cooler parts of the day. Also, watch for rattlesnakes from early spring to late fall.

TAP INTO YOUR CREATIVE SIDE

AT ARTS ON FIRE

When your creative impulses are calling out to you, Arts on Fire, a paint-your-own-pottery studio, offers a lighthearted and encouraging outlet for all ages and experience levels. Pick your mug or plate to paint, or go for a whimsical swan or squirrel or another fun decorative ceramic piece. Even if you have never picked up a brush in the past, the amiable and helpful staff will walk you through the process and offer guidance to make you feel like an expert by the time your piece is painted. Plan on two to three hours, which is why some people bring a bottle of wine and snacks to enjoy with a group of friends. After you finish, the folks at Arts on Fire fire your piece for you and have it ready for pickup four or five days later. Creating something connected with such a good time being together is very satisfying.

200 S 23rd Ave., Ste. A1, 406-586-8081
artsonfirebozeman.com

TIP

If you want something to do for the kids during the summer, check out the Art Camps at Arts on Fire.

WALK WHERE THE RIVERS CONVERGE
AT MISSOURI HEADWATERS STATE PARK

All that remains of Gallatin City, the bustling town that served as the county seat from 1862 to 1867, are the remnants of the hotel built in 1868. Now a more tranquil setting, Missouri Headwaters State Park remains a geological focal point as much today as it was for Indigenous people, explorers, and settlers, offering an opportunity to step away from the crowds in a natural setting. At the campground, you can rent a tepee for the night and spend time where the Lewis and Clark Expedition camped when they were in the area in 1805 and 1806. Sacagawea grew up in the area and assured the expedition members they were on the right route. There are multiple walking trails with informational signs and kiosks to explain the history and geography of the park's 558 acres. Half a mile from the campground is the confluence of the three rivers, and another half mile beyond is a beautiful picnic area with picnic tables underneath the massive cottonwoods.

1585 Trident Rd., 406-285-3610
fwp.mt.gov/stateparks/missouri-headwaters

TIP

Bring your bike and travel the paved 11.8-mile Headwaters Trail System that follows a retired railbed of the Milwaukee Road. The trail runs from near the park office at Missouri Headwaters State Park to the nearby town of Three Forks.

COMPREHEND THE EVOLUTION

OF TECHNOLOGY AT THE AMERICAN COMPUTER AND ROBOTICS MUSEUM

With current technology, we have the world's knowledge at our fingertips. Yet a tour of the American Computer and Robotics Museum shows us the humble beginning of what now allows us to video chat worldwide and explore space. The Computer and Robotics Museum is not a sprawling space but packs in much information. Exhibits demonstrate how, beginning with an original cuneiform stone tablet, developed around 3500 BCE, we have progressed to almost incomprehensible computing technology that fits into our hands. There is a display explaining the Enigma codebreaking machine of World War II, along with exhibits highlighting the development of computers through the decades. Strolling through the exhibits is also a walk down memory lane for those who have used computers their entire lives, as you can view various models of Macs and PCs going back decades. And because technology continually improves, there is a dive into the worlds of artificial intelligence and robotics and what they potentially mean for humanity.

2023 Stadium Dr., #1-A, 406-582-1288
acrmuseum.org

TIP

Take advantage of one of their special events for an in-depth look into everything from a high-tech wine tasting to an up-close look at new robots to a sneak peek at artifacts that still need to be displayed.

EXPERIENCE THE OLD WEST
AT NEVADA CITY AND VIRGINIA CITY

Just over an hour from Bozeman, visit Virginia City, the 1865 capital of the Territory of Montana, where gold brought more than 10,000 hopeful souls to Alder Gulch, the mining area between Virginia City and the nearby mining town Nevada City. Virginia City, which once was home to 5,000 of these hardworking folk, is open throughout the year. Watch a vaudeville performance of the Illustrious Virginia City Players at the Opera House, gear up in Western attire at Ranks Mercantile, or belly up to the Bale of Hay Saloon, established in the 1860s. Don't miss the historical residence of Thomas Francis Meagher, the lively and most-likely murdered first governor of the territory. Take the short drive up to Boot Hill to visit the graves of those hanged by vigilantes, pan for gold, and explore the living history of these former mining towns.

406-843-5247
virginiacitymt.com

TIP

Young and old love the 15-minute ride on the Alder Gulch Shoreline Train, which takes visitors over Alder Creek and through beautiful scenery between Virginia City and Nevada City. The train runs from Memorial Day to Labor Day, and tickets are first come, first served.

FIND YOUR WAY
TO THE HISTORIC CRAIL RANCH

The remaining structures at the Crail Ranch remind us of the hearty nature of the people who built their lives in this rugged area. In 1902, Augustus Frank Crail and his wife Sally purchased this 960-acre ranch to raise sheep and grow Crail Fife, a unique variety of wheat developed to thrive in the short, chilly season of the Gallatin Valley. For half a century, the buildings on the ranch were the only structures as far as the eye could see; of these buildings, only the two-story house and simple cabin remain. Operated by the Big Sky Community Corporation, there are tours on the weekends during July and August and special events throughout the years to allow people to catch a glimpse of what life was like in the area. There are several native plant gardens planted and tended by Grow Wild, and visitors are welcome to explore the grounds and enjoy the peaceful nature of the area.

2100 Spotted Elk Rd., 406-993-2112
bsco.org/crail-ranch-homestead/history-preservation

TIP

Follow GPS directions, as it is a bit disconcerting to navigate through the modern Meadow Village neighborhood in Big Sky in search of historic buildings. But rest assured, you are on the right route!

SNUGGLE AN ALPACA
AT ALPACAS OF MONTANA

Over 20 years ago, Sarah and James Budd began their journey to create Alpacas of Montana with eight alpacas. Now they invite guests to meet their home herd of alpacas and the llamas that serve as guard animals. Sarah and James discovered people are as enamored with the adorable animals almost as much as they are of their apparel. Alpaca fans began stopping on the road to take photos, and the couple thought they should invite them onto the farm for a memorable experience. A tour of Alpacas of Montana goes well beyond a petting-zoo experience. Knowledgeable guides share the background and personalities of individual animals as you walk among them on the beautiful farm that keeps approximately 120 animals. You'll discover the alpacas' South American origin, what it takes to raise them for their fiber, and a glimpse of how the animals interact with each other. There are even multiple opportunities to take group and individual photos with the alpacas.

8255 S Cottonwood Rd., 406-579-4055
alpacasofmontana.com

TIP

There is a fully stocked retail shop on the property for visitors who wish to take home an heirloom-quality piece of clothing to remember their visit.

EXPLORE MYRIAD ART STYLES
AT THE EMERSON CENTER

The Emerson Center for the Arts & Culture has been renowned as the heart of art and culture in Bozeman since the early 1990s, yet the building has been a beacon of learning since its construction in 1920. Designed by prominent architect Fred F. Willson, the original school was fittingly named after Ralph Waldo Emerson, a prominent creative mind of the 19th century, and has since found a new life as a hub of artistic talent. For those looking for a one-of-a-kind gift, Galleria Hall features many talented artists offering their work. Former classrooms are now artists' work studios, galleries, and small businesses where you'll find everything from guitar lessons to art therapy, and the historic Crawford Theater's vintage charm and expansive stage still brings people together for film screenings and live performances.

111 S Grand Ave., 406-587-9797
theemerson.org

TIP

During the summer, for a chance to visit and play in the middle of the day, Lunch on the Lawn brings together food vendors, live music, and kids' activities.

VIEW GRIZZLIES UP CLOSE
AT THE MONTANA GRIZZLY ENCOUNTER

For those who want to safely see a grizzly bear from a close distance, the Montana Grizzly Encounter offers a front-row experience of these magnificent animals that far surpasses a typical zoo visit. The rescued grizzlies are ambassadors of the wild that help educators tell the story of the bears' near extirpation and subsequent successful preservation. To view the bears, book your ticket online and choose your time. (There are no ticket purchases at the facility.) After heading through the gift shop and viewing the adorable Nigerian goats, head to the viewing area to watch the "bear of the hour" spend time in its habitat. Everyone has a terrific view, making this an excellent opportunity for photos, mainly because the bear often plays in the water or with other features of the enclosure. Keeper Talks provides background and education every hour on the half hour. Each grizzly has its own story; their distinct personalities shine. Grab a treat at the snack stand and enjoy a picnic lunch before or after the viewing.

80 Bozeman Hill Rd., 406-586-8893
grizzlyencounter.org

TIP

There are limited hours during the winter, but the Montana Grizzly Encounter is still open because the bears here do not snuggle down for a long nap.

75

SEE HOW BOZEMAN BEGAN
AT THE GALLATIN HISTORY MUSEUM

To truly appreciate an area, it's important to understand the people and events that created it. Stepping through the doors of the Gallatin History Museum, which served as the Gallatin County Jail from 1911 to 1982, is a portal to when Bozeman was a much more rambunctious place. The heavy doors of the jail cells—and the noose hanging from the ceiling—are sober reminders of the severe consequences of pioneer justice. The museum gives us a glimpse of what lives were like for those serving their terms with thoughts and images scratched onto the cell walls by prisoners. Visit the concrete-walled tunnel that runs from the research room, which is filled with original documents and is its own treasure, to the county courthouse as a sure way never to lose a prisoner. Besides the jail features, a small log cabin exhibit shows us what life was like in the wilderness, and there are multiple displays giving us a taste of what Bozeman looked like in the mid to late 1800s.

317 W Main St., 406-522-8122
gallatinhistorymuseum.org

STEP BACK IN TIME
AT THE HEADWATERS HERITAGE MUSEUM

While visiting Three Forks, make a point to spend some time at the Headwaters Heritage Museum to better appreciate the region. Located in the former Three Valley Bank building that was built in 1910, it has been a fixture in the community since 1982. The museum continues to delight and educate residents and visitors with more than 9,000 specimens in its wide variety of exhibits. The friendly staff is always happy to answer questions and share stories. You'll want to take your time with the thousands of items in multiple exhibits highlighting what life was like for Indigenous people, fur traders, pioneers, and those living during the war years. Do not miss their barbed wire collection that features more than 700 pieces and the Fisher Eagle Anvil, the oldest one in Montana. Stepping outside, the cabin behind the museum gives us a perspective on what life was like in this rugged country. It's hard to imagine spending a brutal winter in such close quarters! Peruse their shelves of books for sale to take home a piece of history with you.

202 S Main St., 406-285-4778
tfhistory.org

BONUS MUSEUM IN THREE FORKS

When the Lewis and Clark Expedition floated through the area in 1805, they noted the presence of limestone, a key ingredient in cement manufacture. In 1907, the Three Forks Portland Cement Company was the reason 3,000 people called Trident home, and the depot was built in 1911 by the Northern Pacific Railroad. A century later, volunteers saved the structure and moved it via truck to Three Forks, where it welcomes visitors to marvel at the productivity of these intrepid settlers.

Headwaters Railroad
and Trident Heritage Center
tfhistory.org

77

GHOST HUNT
WITH BOZEMAN PARANORMAL SOCIETY

With Bozeman's colorful past, it's no surprise that some spirits choose to hang around during a walking tour with the Bozeman Paranormal Society. The intrepid team takes guests throughout downtown Bozeman with the latest ghost-hunting gear to see what, or who, they might find. A few of the favorite locations include the Rialto, where the Puerto Rican baritone and beloved Bozeman resident who passed in 2000, Pablo Elvira, seems to enjoy being around people and the performances. Another outing includes hiking in Bear Canyon, where the spirit of a young girl sometimes appears. From the most likely accounts, she was the daughter of a gentleman who owned a logging company in the area, and she accidentally fell into the nearby river and drowned. Although stories circulated that she lures women into the woods, the Bozeman Paranormal Society team reports her as a friendly ghost who yearns for company. Because Montana is a hot spot for UFO sightings, they also spend a few beautiful summer evenings scanning the night skies for unknown objects along with the spectacular astronomical displays.

406-580-8855
facebook.com/BozemanParanormal

DISCOVER YOUR PASSION
AT THE BOZEMAN ART MUSEUM

Surrounded by natural beauty, the Bozeman Art Museum brings a feeling of wonder to its visitors. Continually changing exhibits feature prominent styles ranging from Charles M. Russell to Picasso or the fantasy and adventure Korshak Collection, along with regionally specific art displays. The Bozeman Art Museum offers opportunities for everyone, including over 1,400 school-aged children each year, to answer the call to create. There are many classes for kids and adults, from learning how to utilize flowers for natural dying, painting with watercolors, needle felting, and so many more. Look for the relaxed and fun MAP Brewery Sip and Paint classes, where participants learn techniques while enjoying a pint. In other events, artists venture into the area's marvelous natural spaces for the Plein Air Montana program, where they paint in regions throughout the Gallatin Valley and then display them in a month-long exhibit, along with quick draws at local fishing access sites.

2612 W Main St., 406-570-1419
bozemanartmuseum.org

TIP

Their current space is between the Frugal Frame Shop and Distinctive Lighting, but the grand plan is to build a stand-alone facility that is the hub of the art community.

GROW WILD
AT THE BIG SKY WILDFLOWER FESTIVAL

Immerse yourself in the beautiful native landscape during the Big Sky Wildflower Festival in the first half of July. The Crail Ranch Historical Museum, where the group designed and installed native and locally adapted plant gardens to show off the potential of this type of landscape, is the home base for many of the festival events. During these flower-focused activities, choose workshops such as nature photography, watercolor painting at the gardens, flower arranging, or more creative ways to connect with the flowers. For fun, they also have a "Noxious Weed Bouquet" contest at the Big Sky Farmers Market, where stopping to pick the flowers benefits everyone. The festival packs in hikes, talks, and the excellent camaraderie that defines Grow Wild, a nonprofit organization dedicated to preserving the native landscape. Even beyond this special event, they strive to protect and enhance the plants that connect the ecosystem through various events and projects.

903 N Black Ave., 406-209-0905
growwildmt.org

TIP

To keep up the beneficial work at any time of the year, fill out a volunteer form to help the team pull weeds on public land to improve wildlife habitat.

VISIT THE UNDERWORLD
OF THE LEWIS AND CLARK CAVERNS

From May 1 until September 30, a Montana Fish, Wildlife & Parks guide leads visitors through the largest known limestone caverns in the Northwest. The twisting labyrinth can be challenging, but two different tours help meet fitness levels. The two-hour-long Classic Tour is the more difficult route that takes guests on a two-mile journey down more than 500 steps, sliding down wet rocks, squeezing through tight spaces, and climbing 300 feet. While visiting the Cathedral Room, the Pit, Garden of the Gods, the Brown Waterfall Room, and Paradise, the guide talks about the geological and human history of the area. It gives guests a thrill after everyone turns off their flashlights. There is also a more accessible mile-long tour that is ideal for kids or anyone who is a bit claustrophobic. Purchase tickets either in person or online. If you're in the area during the latter part of December, purchase a ticket for a memorable Candlelight Tour experience exploring part of the caverns holding candle lanterns.

25 Lewis & Clark Caverns Rd., Whitehall, 406-287-3541
fwp.mt.gov/stateparks/lewis-and-clark-caverns

TIP

Bring a jacket on any of the tours. Even though it might be over 90 degrees outside, the interior temperature hovers around 50 degrees with 90 percent humidity, so it feels cold!

Guitars at Music Villa

SHOPPING AND FASHION

SUPPORT LOCAL PRODUCERS
AT THE BOZEMAN FARMERS MARKET

The Bozeman Farmers Market brings the finest local producers and talented craftspeople to Lindley Park every Tuesday from 5 to 8 p.m. from the second half of June through mid-September. Montana, and particularly the Gallatin Valley, offers some of the most impressive food in the world, and we are fortunate to find it all in one place at this weekly social gathering. Stroll through the serene, shaded Lindley Park to grab the highest-quality groceries, including fresh fruits and vegetables, meat, eggs, regional cheeses, mushrooms, cider, and baked goods for weekly menus. Artisans and craftspeople draw inspiration to create beautiful and functional pieces, making this an ideal time to shop for others—or yourself. Enjoy local musicians as you find the perfect handcrafted items in this weekly celebration of summer.

Lindley Park
E Main St. and Buttonwood Ave.
bozemanfarmersmarket.org

TIP

Plan on having dinner at the market, as well. With so many food and drink options, you can easily try something different each week throughout the season.

DIG INTO FASCINATING NATURAL HISTORY ITEMS AT EARTH'S TREASURES

For anyone with an affinity for rock hounding, fossils, or the natural world, head to Earth's Treasures. This place offers genuine megalodon or mammoth teeth, fossilized sea life, and even pyritized ammonites. Unique stones and minerals enthusiasts will delight in the large selection of natural specimens, along with polished and shaped gems. Earth's Treasures showcases many Montana-specific varieties, including Hyalite opals, crystals from the renowned digging area Crystal Park near Dillon, and our state gems, Montana agates and Yogo sapphires. For the true naturalist in the family, framed butterflies and insects serve as the perfect gift to display their passion for the study of this subject. Intense amethyst geodes, glittering agate slices, and other stone decor add a conversation piece to any home. This is the place to discover one-of-a-kind items and rock-minded friends.

25 N Willson Ave., 406-586-3451
earthstreasuresmt.com

TIP

If you want to try your hand at gold panning and looking for gems, Earth's Treasures is the place to go for rockhounding supplies and prospecting advice.

AID GRIZZLY CONSERVATION

AND RENT BEAR SPRAY AT HEY BEAR

Understanding how to handle a grizzly bear encounter is essential for anyone who wants to explore the outdoors in Montana. Hey Bear's mission is to educate recreationists and offer unique merchandise that helps them looks good. Every winter and summer, Hey Bear releases a new collection of hats, shirts, and outerwear to raise awareness about our relationship with this symbol of the wild. They also provide dog accessories, such as beefy leather Hey Bear–stamped collars, and nifty items like SCAT belts for carrying bear spray and your phone. It is very convenient that Hey Bear rents bear spray to visitors and teaches them how to use it. The staff excels in proper bear etiquette, whether you are day hiking or spending nights in the wilderness. The staff holds educational programs on what to do in case of an encounter and the importance of preserving grizzlies for future generations.

11 Lone Peak Dr., Unit #104
heybear.com

TIP

You do not have to return your can of bear spray only to the Big Sky office. They have drop boxes throughout Big Sky, Bozeman, and Yellowstone National Park.

SHINE
AT MONTANA SILVERSMITHS

Montana's state motto, "Oro y Plata"—Gold and Silver—inspired many people to flock to the Treasure State over 150 years ago. Today we discover these glittering treasures at Montana Silversmiths. The artisans at Montana Silversmith are renowned for their intricately designed trophy belt buckles for world-class rodeo champions, capturing public interest with their beautiful craftsmanship. They continue to provide these sought-after trophy buckles for the Professional Bull Riders, National Finals Rodeo, and the Calgary Stampede, and are equally renowned for crafting exceptional jewelry pieces for those of us who have never spent eight seconds on the back of a bronc. They offer rings, bracelets, necklaces, and earrings in designs that suit every style, with each piece elegantly fashioned as a reminder of Montana. Because gemstones and silver go beautifully together, Montana Silversmith artists pair turquoise and other natural gemstones with shining silver, giving the jewelry a distinctly Western feel.

14 W Main St., 406-404-1080
montanasilversmiths.com

TIP

Montana Silversmiths will happily create items for special occasions, such as weddings, births, or family reunions as memorable pieces that are sure to be handed down for generations.

BUZZ INTO
MONTANA HONEY BEE COMPANY

Montana ranks as one of the top honey producers in the country, and the Montana Honey Bee Company serves as a perfect home base for hobbyist beekeepers and those who adore the honey bee aesthetic. Combining practicality and style, half of the shop features bee equipment, including Langstroth and top bar hives, bee suits, veils, smokers, and other necessary beekeeping accessories. For those who want to delve into this fascinating hobby, the knowledgeable crew at the Montana Honey Bee Company offers classes throughout the year and provides a solid community for new beekeepers. Honey is the heart of the store, and the Montana Honey Bee Company offers a wide selection of varietal honey from across the country, such as Tupelo honey, a rich, florally sweet honey from the Georgia–Florida region, along with Montana-produced honey in liquid or creamed forms. You'll also find local bee pollen, beeswax-based salves and lotions, and bee-inspired home decor.

19 S Tracy Ave., 406-624-6446
montanahoneybeecompany.com

86

LOOK FOR THE PERFECT HAT AND BOOTS
AT HEAD WEST

The sweet, earthy smell of leather lets you know you're in the right place to discover your Bozeman style. Head West features a wide selection of Western clothing. High-quality Stetson and Head West Private Label felt hats are a functional fashion statement. The dark brown Bozeman hat is ideal for any Western traveler because the dense structure of the wool makes it durable and weather resistant. You can shove it in your backpack when you don't need it. Whether you're attending the rodeo or hitting the dance floor, boots are a must-have accessory, and Head West offers a wide range of styles and materials. Their eye-catching ostrich leather boots boast dyed leather and added features like fringe and turquoise. The folks at Head West will help you find the perfect fit, such as a Hyer Boot for a night on the dance floor, or slip on a more practical Stetson Rancher Zip Boot for day-to-day use.

111 E Main St., 406-585-3322
rockymountaintoycompany.com

TIP

Although known for their Western apparel, Head West also has heirloom-quality Pendleton blankets and a fine selection of home and gift items.

87

DECK OUT YOUR BACKCOUNTRY WARDROBE
WITH SITKA GEAR

Bozeman-based SITKA Gear, a world-renowned designer and manufacturer of high-performance outdoor apparel, offers clothing and equipment that combine functionality and fashion at their flagship store. The spacious, open-concept space feels immense with its high ceilings supported by rustic wood beams, fitting for the quest to find clothing that works for the Montana terrain. For years, people have viewed SITKA as one of the top brands for outfitting hunters and outdoor-minded clients because it uses the most technologically advanced materials, such as Gore-Tex, Windstopper, and PrimaLoft (a synthetic insulating material that keeps you warm even when it becomes wet), to create top-quality apparel and gear that lasts a lifetime. Extensive research and field testing ensure that cutting-edge ideas translate into real-world practicality in terms of comfort and durability. More recently, SITKA has applied this attention to detail to a daily wear line of clothing for men and women, creating clothing suitable for tamer pursuits.

1251 N Rouse Ave., 406-522-5900
sitkagear.com

TIP

SITKA Gear also provides in-house repairs to back their guarantee of quality and durability and to fix typical wear because people love and want to hold onto this equipment.

FIND THE PERFECT GIFT
AT HEYDAY

When you need a gift for someone in your life or a treat for yourself, head to Heyday. The creative sales staff has curated a selection to match any occasion. There are books, plush animals, and unique crafting items for the kids, such as heart ring crayons, which might be equally fun as an adult gift! Grown-ups will appreciate their high-quality home goods, candles, body care products, jewelry, and book selections, particularly the inspiring cookbooks. And not to be left out, there are gifts for the guys ranging from beard balm to a single-serving margarita mix that is perfect for tossing in the backpack. This open and bright store has a comfortable, homey atmosphere that encourages you to browse. The best part is that even when gift shopping can be stressful, their friendly and helpful staff are happy to offer recommendations for everyone, from pet lovers to skiers or those who want to take home a special reminder of Montana.

7 W Main St., 406-586-5589
heydaybozeman.com

STEP INTO THE IDEAL OUTDOOR BOOT
AT SCHNEE'S

Visiting Schnee's flagship store in the historic brick building built in 1903 on the corner of East Main Street and North Black Avenue is a reminder that Schnee's Boots have a long history in Bozeman and Montana. They feature the handcrafted Schnee's brand boots, suitable for any condition Montana throws at you, along with plenty of additional footwear brands, such as Oboz and Hoka, highly reputable brands for hiking and general outdoor activities. Even their lineup of everyday clothing combines form and function, adding style while maintaining a reputation for high quality. The best part of visiting the store is that the sales team's expertise matches the quality of their merchandise, and they are more than happy to help you figure out what will work best for your activity, including offering Mystery Ranch backpacks and any outdoor gear needed for camping or hiking adventures.

35 E Main St., 406-920-3413
schnees.com

TIP

For the true hunting fans, step into the firearms room where you'll find taxidermied specimens from throughout Africa and North America, along with an impressive selection of shotguns and rifles.

BE DAZZLED
AT ZSA-ZSA'S

You know you're in the right place when an enormous, brilliantly purple amethyst geode greets you at the entrance. Raised in Gdańsk, Poland, proprietor Joanna Pratt calls Bozeman her home. Setting out from here, she travels the world to bring back unique geological specimens that "tickle her soul" as jewelry and home decor. Beautifully lit and displayed, the natural crystals bring a sense of peace to her shop. Three- to five-foot-tall fluorite tower lamps stand with a beautiful glow, and stunningly smooth onyx bowls are an ideal natural feature in any earth-centered home. With a keen eye for beauty, she ethically sources collector pieces such as full-size Lemurian quartz and amethyst angel wings. Crystals are the heart of Zsa-Zsa's, and Joanna offers loose amber from her home city, which is well known for this stunning gemstone, as well as exquisite turquoise, malachite, moonstone, and nearly any crystal your heart desires in pendants, rings, and permanent jewelry. If it sparkles, it truly shines at Zsa-Zsa's.

23 W Main St., 307-250-0227
zsa-zsas.com

CUDDLE UP WITH YOUR FAVORITE READ
AT THE COUNTRY BOOKSHELF

The cavernous Country Bookshelf, where rows upon rows of books offer unlimited delight, is a bibliophile's happy place. Founded in 1957, the Country Bookshelf is the largest independent bookstore in Montana and the region's literary hub. Montana has a long history as a home for writers, and besides featuring an impressive section of regional authors, they regularly organize in-person events featuring writers and their works, along with open mic nights for local poets. Shelves are teeming with books, and the staff generously offers recommendations posted on notes stuck near their favorite books throughout the store. It's all about community and connection, and even if you have yet to decide what you want to read, there's nothing better than chatting with enthusiastic staff members who love nothing more than sharing their passion for a good book.

28 W Main St., 406-587-0166
countrybookshelf.com

TIP

Beyond books, the Country Bookshelf is the place to pick up the perfect card for a special occasion, along with sketchbooks and notebooks to record your journey or daily thoughts.

92

BRING HOME MONTANA FLARE
AT THE MONTANA GIFT CORRAL

Montana Gift Corral rounds up a wide selection of Montana-themed items for those looking for that perfect gift to remember their Montana visit. The beautiful, bricked store is an ample, well-organized, welcoming space. Bring home the flavor of the region with buffalo jerky or elk summer sausage. Huckleberries are hugely popular in Montana, and the Montana Gift Corral offers flapjack mix, syrup, jams, jellybeans, and coffee and tea. There are also home decor items, including locally made pottery and whimsical black bear pieces from Montana creator Jeff Fleming of Bear Country Gallery. For easy-to-pack gifts, they have Montana-made jewelry, books by Montana authors, Montana-inspired clothing, plus bath and body products. Huckleberry soap is always a big hit. For those who have the Christmas spirit throughout the year, the Christmas corner offers candles, artwork, and ornaments you'll find nowhere else.

237 E Main St., 406-898-2034
giftcorral.com

TIP

The creative staff are experts in creating the best gift basket, and they are happy to ship your items.

SHOP FOR LOCAL FLAVOR
AT BOZEMAN COMMUNITY FOOD CO-OP

The Co-op is far more than a grocery store. It is a local and sustainable food experience. The flagship store on West Main Street is a high-quality culinary utopia with a helpful and friendly staff that makes you feel like family. You can become a lifetime member for extra savings, but the co-op welcomes everyone. Their cheese selection offers regional, artisanal cheeses, such as chevre from Amaltheia Organic Dairy located in Belgrade, plus it's possible to find gjetost cheese from Norway and a Swiss Kaltbach Gruyère (the secret ingredient for making the best homemade mac and cheese). Their meat department has a wide selection of Montana-produced beef, lamb, and pork, but don't skip the gorgeous produce area stocked with locally grown fruits and vegetables. They also pride themselves on using regionally produced flour, eggs, and dairy in their breads and pastries baked on location. It's a treat to wander the aisles and experience regional food at its finest.

908 W Main St., 406-587-4039
bozo.coop

TIP

Both the main store and the downtown location on East Main feature self-serve delis with packed salad bars, as well as hot and cold dishes.

MATCH THE HATCH
AT YELLOW DOG FLYFISHING

Whether you are new to fly-fishing or are looking for high-quality gear for a local adventure, Yellow Dog Flyfishing has you covered. When it comes to fly rods, they carry the classic dry fly rods, along with spey and Euro-nymphing rods, offering an exceptional tool in targeting wily trout. From supplies like reels and leaders and tippets to instruction on the perfect fly for every time of the season, they provide you with everything you need for a memorable time on the river. Of course, this includes the right gear to wear, as anyone who has spent time chasing fish knows that Mother Nature doesn't always play nice. In reality, sometimes the best days for fishing are not the nicest ones to be standing outside, yet it is fine when you have the right outerwear. Yellow Dog offers high-quality waders, along with shirts for every weather occasion, rain gear, insulated jackets, gloves, and hats.

81801 Gallatin Rd., 406-585-8667
yellowdogflyfishing.com

TIP

The staff at Yellow Dog Flyfishing all love fly-fishing and are happy to offer advice on gear and where to go for your best chance of success. Stop back to tell them how you did!

FIND THAT FUNKY MUSIC
AT CACTUS RECORDS & GIFTS

Affectionately dubbed the "Weirdo Store," comical vibes rule at Cactus Records. While that description is the best short answer describing what they offer, there is so much more! Where else can you find a blow-up unicorn? It's worth the time to browse and chuckle at their collection of novelties in the selection of cards, magnets, stickers, banners, jewelry, hats, and apparel—because everyone needs a pair of Cheech & Chong socks. Leaving the store without laughing at one of their whacky items is impossible. The music is the store's heart and part of the reason it's been around for over 50 years. Vinyl takes center stage at Cactus Records, although they also offer CDs and cassette tapes. You're sure to find famous artists as well as plenty of obscure albums you didn't even know you needed. To spin those records, they sell turntables, and the friendly staff is more than happy to talk music with you.

2742 W Main St., 406-587-0245
cactusrecords.net

TIP

If you're looking for an upcoming music venue, check out their website, or better yet, come to the store to peruse the flyers to see who is playing locally. They occasionally feature live music in the store for special events.

DELIGHT THE KIDS
AT THE GREAT ROCKY MOUNTAIN TOY COMPANY

After seeing all the marvelous sights around Bozeman, the youngsters will be thrilled to stop at the Great Rocky Mountain Toy Company. Expect wide eyes when babies and big kids (of all ages!) step into this world of wonder. There are few other places to find a badger plushy, and babies can cuddle the stuffed animals or happily play with the colorful and safe sensory toys for their quickly developing brains. Older kids can check out the LEGO blocks, Breyer Horses, Rubik's Cubes, and various games for the family. Outdoor activities, such as a kids' pickleball set, a cornhole outfit, dart boards, street hockey, and even a backyard zip line, are just a handful of the family fun possibilities. Play is learning, and the Great Rocky Mountain Toy Company offers physics and chemistry kits, telescopes, and even Sea-Monkeys to sharpen young, quizzical minds. Step into their darkened nook with glow-in-the-dark and space-related items for a magical experience.

111 E Main St., 406-585-3322
rockymountaintoycompany.com

TIP

They have a sister store in Big Sky at 145 Town Center Avenue, Unit A2, so you can pick up a toy or two while visiting that area.

JAM AT THE LEGENDARY MUSIC VILLA

Music Villa is Shangri-La for those who are serious about playing music! As you step inside, gleaming electric guitars of every shape, color, and style line the walls, and rows at your fingertips invite you to ask for a cable and plug it into an amp. Their acoustic selection is impressive, and with the Gibson acoustic facility in Bozeman, Music Villa is front and center for the newest arrivals of these renowned, handcrafted guitars. Their Villa Vault room features the premier electric and acoustic guitar styles in vintage and one-of-a-kind models that collectors seek. Yet Music Villa accommodates all euphonic interests, including banjos, mandolins, drums, and keyboards, along with orchestral instruments such as violins, upright basses, and cellos. If you need an accessory, they undoubtedly have it, plus they have a professional-level inventory on the electronics end for amps, mixing consoles, and recording equipment.

539 E Main St., 406-587-4761
musicvilla.com

TIP

If playing a musical instrument is a new endeavor for you, the talented crew at Music Villa offers lessons online and in person for many of the instruments.

GEAR UP FOR BACKCOUNTRY ADVENTURES
AT UPHILL PURSUIT

When Nature beckons, make Uphill Pursuit your first stop. The experienced team has the technical gear for everything from a casual run to skirting the Bridger Mountains, overnight camping trips, multiday backpacking adventures, not to mention backcountry skiing and bicycling, including bike-packing, excursions. If it has to do with the outdoors, they have you covered. The best part is that their staff are the folk you are likely to see on the trails or climbing ice in the dead of winter. They are more than happy to share their experiences with wide ranges of gear to offer recommendations that best fit your needs, especially when bringing every piece of gear to an area is not possible. Uphill Pursuit also has an extensive rental program for backcountry skiing and ice climbing, including beacons, shovels, and probes for avalanche safety. To be able to communicate with those at home base, they also rent Garmin In-Reach mini satellite communication systems to ensure a safe experience.

211 E Oak St., Ste. 1D, 406-404-1021
uphillpursuits.com

TIP

They offer full-service tune-ups and repairs on bicycles, as well as ski equipment so you are ready once the snow flies.

FIND TREASURES
AT ANTIQUE MARKET & MORE

It's impossible to miss the sprawling Antique Market & More just a mile east of Four Corners. Dozens of vendors bring in new items nearly daily, and you're sure to find decor for any flair, along with vintage signs and advertising. Stepping through the doors of this antique shop always leads to fascinating finds. Take time to peruse the dozens of booths from regional dealers who spend hours searching for treasures just for you! Many of the vendors specialize in Western decor, and you are bound to find Native-inspired pieces such as turquoise jewelry, handcrafted beadwork, or vintage leatherwork. It can be challenging to find antique furniture in the West, but Antique Market & More has a wide selection of matching and individual pieces. Whether you need an antique medicine bottle or a life-size bronze, you'll find it at Antique Market & More.

8332 Huffine Ln., 406-586-0985
antiquemarketandmore.com

TIP

Visit the Antique Barn near Gallatin Gateway and discover a mix of old furniture and collectibles, along with newer items and reclaimed pieces.

5 Wheeler Mountain Way, 406-763-4676
antiquebarn.net

STEP BACK IN TIME
AT BOZEMAN VINTAGE

Bozeman Vintage results from a lifelong pursuit to rediscover the cool, weird stuff that makes your heart happy. If you have fond memories of a favorite style, you will undoubtedly find it here. Denim in every conceivable version and custom-altered pieces make the apparel genuinely one of a kind. Look for your favorite era of jeans, jackets, gabardine shirts, eye-catching belt buckles, authentic Western-wear Levis, Wrangler items, and well-worn Carhartt jackets. Don't forget the cowboy hats and boots that have probably seen a thing or two on the ranch or the dance floor. Half the joy of this eclectic shop is perusing their carefully curated selection of broad Americana, including key chains from long-defunct hotels, political buttons, novelty ashtrays that were all the rage in the '70s, and costume jewelry. Step inside for the memories and take a tangible piece of them home.

1008 N 7th Ave., Unit F, 406-595-4305
bozemanvintage.com

La Châtelaine Chocolat Co.

ACTIVITIES
BY SEASON

WINTER

SPRING

SUMMER

FALL

SUGGESTED ITINERARIES

INDOOR ACTIVITIES FOR THE KIDS

OUTDOOR ACTIVITIES FOR THE KIDS

FIND YOUR FAVORITE OUTDOOR ADVENTURE

EPIC DATE DAY

MUSIC AND ART ADVENTURES

EXPLORE THE GALLATIN VALLEY'S COLORFUL HISTORY

GIRLS' OUTING

GUYS' NIGHT OUT

DAY TRIPS FROM BOZEMAN

A SHORT STAY IN BOZEMAN

INDEX